NEW AIMS IN CHILDREN'S LITERATURE

Leland B. Jacobs, General Editor

The Child as Critic

The Child as Critic

Teaching Literature in the Elementary School

Glenna Davis Sloan

TEACHERS COLLEGE PRESS
TEACHERS COLLEGE, COLUMBIA UNIVERSITY
NEW YORK AND LONDON

Library of Congress Cataloging in Publication Data

Sloan, Glenna Davis, 1930-
    The child as critic.

    Bibliography: p.
    1. Literature—Study and teaching (Elementary)
2. Language arts (Elementary) I. Title.
LB1575.S53   372.6'4   75-23360
ISBN 0-8077-2482-3

The publisher and the author gratefully acknowledge these copyright owners and publishers for their permission to reprint the following selections:

"Swing Song" from *The Little Hill* by Harry Behn. Copyright 1949 by Harry
    Behn. Reprinted by permission of Harcourt Brace Jovanovich, Inc.
"When my canary" from *Cricket Songs: Japanese Haiku.* Translated and
    copyright 1964 by Harry Behn. Reprinted by permission of Harcourt
    Brace Jovanovich, Inc., and Curtis Brown, Ltd.
"Dark Girl" from *Personals* by Arna Bontemps. Copyright 1963 by Arna
    Bontemps. Reprinted by permission of Harold Ober Associates, Inc.
"A City Park" from *A Family Album and Other Poems* by Alter Brody.
    Copyright 1918 by B. W. Huebsch, Inc. and renewed 1946 by Alter
    Brody. Reprinted by permission of The Viking Press, Inc.
"Wild Geese" by Elinor Chipp. Reprinted by permission of Branden Press,
    Inc.
"I Am" by Hilda Conkling. Copyright 1920 and renewed 1948 by Hilda
    Conkling. Reprinted by permission of Random House, Inc.
"The Goblin" from *Picture Rhymes from Foreign Lands* by Rose Fyleman.
    Copyright 1935 and renewed 1963 by Rose Fyleman. Reprinted by
    permission of J. B. Lippincott Company and The Society of Authors
    as the literary representative of the Estate of Rose Fyleman.
"Transcontinent" by Donald Hall. Reprinted by permission of the author.

To Jake, Charles and Mark

General Editor's Introduction

From the beginnings of elementary education on this continent, literature has had a place in the curriculum. Though frequently used as motivation for other content or exploited to moralistic or character-development ends, nonetheless story and poem have been recognized as important in the school experience of boys and girls.

In this book, Glenna Davis Sloan makes a case for literature for children on its own terms. She goes well beyond many of the traditional proposals for literature in the elementary school. She recognizes that one cannot, strictly speaking, "teach literature." One can make literature available to children either by reading to or with them or by their reading on their own. But once the child has the story or poem in mind—has experienced it—he has what he has made of the prose fiction or verse. What then can one teach?

Dr. Sloan says that then one helps the children to become critics, to the end that they develop their "educated imaginations." But to get to the practices that help children become critics, there must be a theoretical construct espoused. Dr. Sloan accepts Northrop Frye's basic assumptions about what literature is and how it functions in human experience. She interprets his conception of the structural principles of literature and his framework for the criticism of literature.

From such interpretations of Frye's theory, Dr. Sloan clearly shows a goodly variety of classroom activities that foster children's development as critics. In the proposed practices, she relates reading and composing, a most important matter if children are to develop their full potentialities through experiences with literature. Beyond the child's becoming a skillful reader, the school is responsible for teaching the boy or girl to be a critical reader of both informational and literary writing. It is to the latter—the more neglected of the two—that Glenna Davis Sloan so ably makes a much-needed contribution on the following pages.

LELAND B. JACOBS
Professor Emeritus of Education
Teachers College, Columbia University

Foreword

This book is an attempt to explain what the real place of literature is in primary education. Its place is to provide the verbal element in the training of the imagination. The imagination is not a self-indulgent, ornamental, or escapist faculty: it is the constructive power of the mind. Hence one should teach reading neither efficiently nor passively: reading has to be a continuously active and leisurely growth, as all genuine growth is. Because it is active, the teaching of writing is inseparably a part of the teaching of reading, and the aim of teaching a child to write poetry is not to produce poets, but to produce articulate people, articulateness being the highest form of freedom that society can give to the individual. Mrs. Sloan quotes Kenneth Koch, who should know, as remarking that teaching children to write in this way is not really "teaching," in the limited sense, so much as a matter of allowing them to discover and exploit what they already have.

The author makes clear from the beginning her opposition to what she calls the "skills and drills" approach, which frustrates and stunts all genuine imaginative growth. Emphasis on skills tries to be efficient: it regards learning to read as a largely mechanical operation, to be taught with the least waste of time by repetition of familiar words, adding new words gradually as facility is gained. The argument for such teaching seems extremely plausible, and has only the flaw that the human mind, which always begins as a child's mind, is simply not built that way. Consequently such an approach is not merely immoral and anti-intellectual, it is also miserably inefficient, even in its own terms. Emphasis on drills is, again, an emphasis on a "teaching" process in which the teacher is the active agent, the one who knows, and the students are passive, learning through a mechanism of imitation. That doesn't work either.

I have had no firsthand experience with education below the university level, and while I believe that no theory of criticism is any good at all unless it can be adapted to kindergarten and grade one, I naturally make mistakes when I try to suggest how such an adaptation could proceed. I think most of my mistakes have really been much the same mistake: the mistake of underestimating what a child can respond to. Mrs. Sloan, with more experience, does not make this mistake. She knows that children can respond to tragedy and irony as well as to comedy and romance, and that children want difficulty: if they are practicing jumping over hurdles, they want the highest hurdle they can possibly get over, not a low one that they know they can manage. The author also makes it clear that the notion of there being some danger of distorting "reality" by introducing fantasy and myth to the small child is pure (except that it is very impure) superstition. Such dangers only arise in certain types of bad realism. As C. S. Lewis remarks, no child is going to confuse *Alice in Wonderland* with reality, but a pseudo-realistic story about life in a British public school might lead him to expect that school life really was like this. Mrs. Sloan notes that there is now a fashion for realism in children's stories, probably because there is also a fashion for fantasy in adult stories, and adults tend to expect children to make up for their own deficiencies.

When I was about ten I once had to mind the little boy next door, who was about three. He wanted to know what the flowers in the front yard were. I told him they were hydrangeas, and this word, which came out something like "hyainzuz," he repeated all afternoon, chuckling to himself at intervals. Many years later I realized that I had confronted that afternoon one of the primary phenomena of literary education. It is the rare magic word, the mysterious polysyllabic word, that is most likely to become the educational focus, the beckoning light ahead: similarly, it is the magic story, not the imaginatively squalid story, that is most likely to start the quest for awareness going. Ultimately, everyone exposed to literary education has to try to become a Prospero, otherwise he becomes a Caliban. From the stuttering Dick-and-Jane readers to the foul-mouthed blither of the Watergate transcripts, we realize how many Calibans there are who are quite right in saying:

> You taught me language; and my profit on't
> Is, I know how to curse.

But there are still some Prosperos who have learned how to control the magic of words and make it part of their own experience, and it is to increase their number in society that the present book is devoted.

NORTHROP FRYE

Preface

So often, at every level from grade school to college, the study of literature is fragmented. We read this poem, that play, these novels, and examine each as a separate entity. The examination too frequently ends only in cruel vivisection of a work or endless commentary on some aspects of its content. Both as a student and as a teacher I found this fragmentation and subsequent dilution of the power of literature disappointing and unsatisfying. If students are to experience the full impact of literature, they have to encounter it as a cumulative study that adds up to more than a list of apparently unconnected poems and stories. For this to be possible, literary study has to be set within the framework of a theory of literature.

Northrop Frye, the eminent literary critic, has provided such a theory with his delineation of the structural principles of literature and his formulation furnishes the basis for the literary study described in this book. The practice set forth here shows that the study of literature is indeed a cumulative one and that significant beginnings may be made in it in the elementary school, with materials and methods appropriate for use with young children.

The Child as Critic is intended for teachers, prospective teachers, language arts supervisors, designers of curriculum, and others interested in the teaching of English in the elementary school. It combines theory and practice in the belief that effective practice can only be developed where there is a theoretical understructure of consequence. This book proposes a way of unifying the language arts in a program that makes literature the center of language studies. In this proposal literary study is broadly conceived to include both the experiencing of literature and a variety of responses to it, verbal and nonverbal. The primary aim of the program is to foster genuine literacy, something that develops out of a love for language and an awareness of its infinite possibilities, both out-growths of an abundance of pleasurable experiences with fine literature.

Why is it important that young children study literature? What is involved in the study? How exactly do you "teach" literature? What can be done in the elementary school to prepare children for advanced literary studies? These are some of the questions that *The Child as Critic* endeavors to answer.

There are many valid reasons why literature should be part of a child's education; Chapter 1 reviews two of the most important. Chapter 2 is concerned with a definition central to the book: what it means to "teach" and "study" literature. Chapters 3 and 4 provide the foundation of literary theory necessary for the development of learning sequences that will lead to significant literary under-standings. Educational and literary theory are translated into practice in Chapters 5 through 7 where numerous examples of teaching strategies may be found. These include specifics related to planning lessons designed to foster literary understandings; details as to procedures, such as discussion techniques; and suggestions for suitable content to use in learning sequences.

The other side of the coin, composition, is considered here as an integral part of the study of literature, and Chapter 8 details procedures useful in helping children compose stories and poems of their own. Included in the book is an annotated list of selected professional references as well as a bibliography, with page numbers keyed to the text, of all the poems and stories cited. In the case of traditional tales, care was taken to list an outstanding retelling or edition. Students of children's literature will find this bibliography a comprehensive selection of readings in the field.

GLENNA DAVIS SLOAN
Queens College of the
City University of New York

Contents

Chapter 1

The Case for
Literature

Literacy is everyone's concern: educators, parents, employers, and perhaps most of all, the young people who reach high school age with fourth-grade reading skills. In recent years we have seen a proliferation of methods for teaching children to decode printed symbols, the first step in the complex process of becoming an effective, independent reader. The literate person, however, is not one who knows *how* to read, but *one who reads*: fluently, responsively, critically, and because he wants to. Reading involves an engagement with print and an active personal involvement with the ideas expressed in it.

Children will become readers only if their emotions have been engaged, their imaginations stirred and stretched by what they find on printed pages. One way—a sure way—to make this happen is through literature, imaginative literature in particular, where ideally language is used with intensity and power in a direct appeal to the feelings and the imagination. Literature is the most effective "reading program" ever devised.

There are those who shunt literature aside with the argument that elementary education must above all be practical. And since literature addresses itself to the imagination, many teachers can accept it only as a diversion or recreation. It must make way for the more serious business of addressing the reason through down-to-earth instruction in reading. Confronted with low reading-test scores and children who read "below grade level" or not at all, many elementary educators insist that their only legitimate business is

1

the teaching of reading "skills." Too often this means the implementation of a tedious remediation program designed to drill into the child the dullest mechanics of the reading process. For someone who has already learned to hate reading there could hardly be a more futile approach. Drills of skills will not generate interest in reading if none has ever been aroused. Literature nourishes the imagination and develops the desire to read. Children will always be more absorbed in the exploits of Horton the Elephant and Curious George than in the vagaries of long and short vowel sounds.

This is not to say that basic skills need not be taught and developed. But they will be more readily learned and used only if the child, from the earliest age, is continuously made aware that reading is worth his time and attention. Participation in a reading program that does not go beyond drills of skills is like learning to play the piano by practicing scales without ever playing a piece of music.

Nothing is more important or practical in the long run than literature. Nothing should come before it. All efforts to teach reading must begin with it. Literature appeals directly to the emotions and the imagination, carrying within a powerful motivation to participate in its wonders and delights. It is only the *art* of literature that can successfully counter the drawing power of television and mass media.

The slowest learner will profit less from extra doses of dull drill than he will from the injections for the imagination that literature can provide. Furthermore, the ability of the child to experience a story or poem is not dependent upon his ability to decode or read fluently. He, like the telegraph operator, is able to "read" what he hears. Although being read to is not reading for oneself, it is unquestionably the prerequisite for developing a desire to do so.

The Primacy of Poetry

We are constantly told that if we expect instruction to be successful we must begin where the child is. *Imaginative literature is exactly where he is.* Not only are his interests and emotions aroused by it, but it is also closer to his natural mode of expression than other, more utilitarian, uses of language. The imaginative writer, particularly the poet, constantly makes use of analogy and identity, simile and metaphor. So does the child. His thinking and the language that reveals it is characteristically an implied simile: something is like something else in some way.

It is natural for children to make free use of metaphor. A child with a stomach-ache complains that his stomach is "broken." Another looks in awe at his grandmother's varicose veins and asks why her legs are "all thunder and lightning."

In *The Lore and Language of School Children*, Iona and Peter Opie show how children's names for things often come close to poetic expression, at least in the sense of being metaphorical. A boy's mouth is his "cake-hole," his stomach is his "breadbasket," large feet are "beetle crushers." As indicated through their lore and language, children delight in nonsense rhymes, rhythmic chants, riddles, codes, epithets, and all forms of word play or metaphorical use of language. Like the poet, children are fascinated by all the marvelous things that words can do.

The language of poetry is rhythmic and repetitive; so is the natural expression of the child. Movement and language are inextricably bound in children. They are kinesthetic creatures who delight in moving to rhythmical chants made of words that take their fancy. Their natural speech is repetitive, heavily accented, and prolix; given to sing-song, whine, chant, and crooning.

Poetry is a method of thought as well as a means of expression. In many ways it is a primitive method of thought with a logic of its own that has nothing to do with verifiable proofs. The poet has license to say that two quite unlike things are like each other, even that they *are* each other. The prose of the highly advanced technological society with its jargon and high level of abstraction bears little relationship to poetry. We tend to think, since we are surrounded by it, that this prose is the natural way to speak and write. But if prose is more natural than poetry, how is it that the simplest societies create poetry, whereas prose is always a much later and specialized development of civilization?

In simpler societies poetry emerges as a primary need because it is seen as a simple and direct means of expression. In Eskimo, for instance, the word *anerca* means "poetry"; it also means "to breathe." Primitive poetry is linked to movement, to the basic bodily rhythms involved in singing, dancing, and marching. Children, if they are freed to do so, recapitulate the experience of primitive literature. They turn far more easily to the rhythmic, the conventionalized, to riddles, conundrums, and stylized jingles than to the abstract prose of the classroom text. Riddles, where things are described in terms of other things—the very essence of poetic thought—are a special delight.

What child would not be intrigued in figuring out this riddle of a needle and thread?

Old Mother Twitchett has but one eye,
And a long tail which she can let fly;
And every time she goes over a gap,
She leaves a bit of her tail in a trap.

Such poetry and the way of looking at the world that it embodies makes a direct appeal to a child's intellectual excitement. He wants to "guess" and more often than not he guesses quickly and correctly. The mental processes involved in making riddles, proceeding through pun and identification, are very close to a child's own.

We complain that education inhibits spontaneity of expression; it is more likely that a prosaic literary education is the inhibitor. How many times have we found that children treat classroom prose as though it were a dead language, something they try to read and write that bears no relation to the way they speak?

In an attempt to be practical and utilitarian, we ignore the child's natural development. His literary education begins with prose, a prose that is to him nothing more than a foreign language found only in textbooks. Imaginative literature, in particular poetry, is set aside as an extra, to be used as a supplement to the practical program of learning to read and write no-nonsense prose. But poetry *is* a legitimate mode of thought, as legitimate as prose and far more basic.

Figurative language, the staple of poetry and all imaginative literature, is not an embellishment. Figures of speech are not ornaments of thought, not verbal gargoyles, but direct expressions of strong feeling. Without their use our language becomes too abstract and mechanical. Poetry's use of metaphor and visualized imagery makes it a most concrete means of expression. It subordinates logic and sequence to the insights of simile and metaphor.

From rhythmic verse we get a sense of energy and timing, a sense of language disciplined yet filled with a life that evokes a bodily response. An early and pleasurable immersion in poetry—nursery rhymes, jingles, counting songs, rhythmic and imagistic verse of all kinds—is the best introduction to reading and at the same time a defense against literary banality of all kinds. It is also a prerequisite for learning to write.

Good writing has to be based on good speech and good speech is a logical though complex development from natural speech. If we write in a way we never speak our writing is certain to lack conviction and personality. A child's unpunctuated outpourings are neither prose nor poetry but they are *closer* to poetry than to prose. The child, like the primitive poet, seems to understand that verse rather than prose is a simpler and more direct way to conventionalize natural speech. Outside the classroom at least the child's speech is filled with chanting and singing as well as such primitive verse forms as the war-cry and the taunt-song. Hearing verse, speaking it, moving to it is the best way to learn to read and write. For in the verse the child hears echoes of his own speech patterns and feels in his bones rhythms that his body recognizes.

Of course listening to poetry will not by itself teach a child to write. Plenty of practice with appropriate guidance is part of the process (as we shall discuss later). But, as in the development of interest in reading, poetry and other imaginative literature are natural and necessary prerequisites for writing. If we impose alien structures too soon—expecting a child to write practical prose with the mechanical accuracy of a business executive or computer printout—our efforts are doomed to failure. Starting where the child is means knowing where he is and acknowledging it. The prose route to literacy is a rough one as teachers will testify who have to listen to pedestrian basal-reader prose haltingly read and peruse prose offerings that are like essays in a foreign language imperfectly learned.

In the drive toward literacy, we have splintered the subject "English" into a number of discrete entities: reading, listening, speaking, writing, spelling, grammar—each with its own textbooks, drills, exercises, and timetable slots. Reading in particular has often been divorced from the rest of the "language arts," sometimes taught to children by teachers who teach them no other language activity. New knowledge from linguistics and literary criticism indicates the folly of this fragmented approach to language studies. English conceived of in terms of just two components, language and literature, is recognized as a more viable, more holistic, concept. With younger children we are probably best advised to think of English in terms of literature since their intellectual development is largely pre-logical and concerned with imaginative rather than discursive forms of thought. Certainly the fragmented approach to language study has not been particularly effective. It may even be a dangerous and destructive deception, since the view of English as a collection of "communication skills" carries with it the assumption that discursive prose is the point of departure for language learning.

Yet scholars like Ernst Cassirer, Edward Sapir, and Otto Jesperson have confirmed that the essence of language is not communication. The autistic speech of children is one indication that the purely communicative aspect of language has been exaggerated.

Language in the young is much more expressive than utilitarian.

In childhood the conception of reality is subjective and dream-like. Practical associations and all the trappings of reason develop later, toward adolescence. The child grasps analogies that more experienced and practical minds reject as absurd. His mind and senses create relationships foreign to practical thinking. Our advanced society places great value on the practical, prosaic, discursive mode of language and thought. We begin to believe that language began as a utility, that metaphors are merely distortions of fact. Children are not so easily misled. They resist factual prose by refusing to read and write it. They are themselves poets and storytellers, and thrive best on poems and stories.

The experience of literature is a great teacher, but it is not the only one. Efforts to read and write must be guided, channeled, and gradually developed. We know that what is learned is always more important than what is taught and that learning takes place when the natural order of things is respected. This order sets the imagination at the center of the child's experience. It is our task to set imaginative literature at the center of his education.

Literature and the Imagination

If literature is essential to the development of readers and writers who are genuinely literate, it is also essential to the education of the child's imagination. We have no standardized tests to measure imagination, but this does not mean that its education can be neglected. It is after all through the imagination that we participate in every aspect of our daily lives: in conversation, in relating to others with sympathy and consideration, in making choices and decisions, in analyzing news reports and the speeches of politicians, in evaluating advertisements and entertainment.

There is no definitive description of the imagination. But we know that this creative and constructive power is not exclusive with the artist or the inventor. Every individual has an imagination. It is not secondary to the intellect or the emotions; it is the very core of them. Its dual nature allows us to take and give, comprehend and create. Children listen with delight to rhymed riddles and create their own; the stories they hear and read are inspiration for original stories in words or pictures. Literature flows from literature.

How can the study of literature help us to imaginative awareness? Like all art it is concerned not so much with reproducing the world we live in as with creating a world we can imagine. Genuine literature is made up of works that are timeless because they deal with basic human concerns. They are full of life but are not necessarily lifelike. The imaginative reality of literature is heightened like action on a stage. Rhythms are more concentrated, imagery is bolder, conventions are more stylized and varied than anything we know in ordinary experience.

The writer of a story or poem constructs a world that is but never was; within each world is an endless range of imaginative possibilities. A story is not real life—anything can happen, anything goes. Literature illustrates something essential for human beings to realize: that there are no limits for the imagination. Literature makes carpets fly and rabbits talk; it overcomes the tyranny of time and conquers death itself. A Yellow Brick Road leading to an Emerald City will never be found on a road map, but it exists, along with other literary locations, as an imaginative reality.

Furthermore, literature has the capacity to develop our imaginative perspective on reality. What we call reality is a confusing tangle of experience: radios blare at us, advertisers bombard us, we are harassed and hurried, torn in a dozen directions. We have all had the desire, when the confusion of life is at its height, to "get away from it all," "to sort things out," "to see where we are," "to get ourselves together." We feel the need for some perspective on our fragmented experience. One way to get it is through the study of a wide variety of literature, the art that describes not what happens in the historical sense but what happens to human beings as they try to come to terms with living. *Literature gives shape to human experience.*

It also calls forth something from our own imaginative experience, something we "have always known" but couldn't express until literature put it into words and images for us. Thus literature puts us in touch with our own imaginative powers. Nothing is more important for creating a truly human world than realizing the power of our imagination. William Blake said that nothing is real beyond the imaginative patterns we make of reality. Imagination, in Blake's sense, *creates* reality. In the real world there can be no change or reform of any kind unless we first use our imaginations to describe what sort of world we want to build, the kind of life we want to lead.

All our beliefs and actions take shape around a social vision constructed by the imagination. Literature, verbal structures constructed by the power of the imagination, provides us with the means of comprehending and evaluating *all* the verbal structures that confront us: in textbooks, on television, in the speeches of politicians. Literature's use of words (as opposed to the use of words in propaganda) is disinterested. It presents cultural mythology—the important beliefs and concerns that inform our culture—with detachment.

The Adventures of Huckleberry Finn is "just a story" and we enjoy it for that. But it also reveals certain truths of American cultural mythology, history, and social life. What we believe in, what we say we believe in, what we believe is important—all our cultural mythology—is revealed in what are first and foremost good stories worth telling again and again. They express our myths: of the hero who conquered a wilderness with his axe and his gun, of the poor boy who achieves success through hard work, or our belief in continual progress toward "better" things. The myths that inform our culture exist in their purest forms in literature. They are there to be examined first as simple forms of human creativity.

Those who wish to influence others, for good or evil, make use of the same myths we find in literature: pastoral myths, hero myths, sacrificial myths, quest myths. The politician promises to take us back "to the good old days." The advertiser lures us with the promise of a vacation retreat "away from it all," or promises to make rugged heroes of those who eat the right breakfast food. The newspaper editorial shatters the reputation of one man to make a case for the political candidate it supports. The student who has encountered the genuine form of a myth in literature will be less likely to fall prey to its perverted form in the advertisement. He will recognize that the commercial showing the plain and unpopular girl suddenly made pretty and popular by the use of the right face cream is a version of the Cinderella story. He will know that an advertisement showing idealized young men and women kept happy, healthy, and forever youthful by drinking the right kind of cola has stolen its conventions from a literary form: the romance.

Such use of language and myth are part of a social mythology whose purpose is to persuade us to accept—usually for another's gain—the standards and values of the society in which we live. It provides a means of making us adjust to things as they are or as a profiteer would have us believe them to be. Some adjustment to our society is necessary, of course. But it is important to guard against too much passive acquiescence. We cannot fall prey to the illusions that society threatens us with: in propaganda, advertising, or entertainment.

The poet and storyteller on the other hand want nothing from us except a response from our imaginative worlds. Their poems and stories call forth imaginative response; they don't impose it from without. To be aware of one's imaginative social vision is to escape the prison of unconscious social conditioning. Genuine literature, although it may enlighten us, does not set out to teach or preach. Its structures are self-contained worlds that are detached from reality. In contemplating these worlds we develop a capacity for detachment. This capacity can then be carried over to everything in life that attempts to capture the imagination for whatever purpose. The reality of literature is an imaginative reality, surely the most important kind, for it corresponds to something within ourselves. It reminds us that we have an imaginative world of our own, a world of possibilities, that we are capable of freedom and of choice.

Young people require educated imaginations if they are to cope with the social pressures that confront them. A well-developed imagination is their protection against social mythology in all its forms: entertainment, advertising, propaganda, the language of cliche and stereotype, the abstractions of jargon and gobbledegook. In an irrational world the trained reason is important. But a developed imagination is fundamental to the survival of a sane society.

Chapter 2

A New Approach
to Literature

Literacy is not something that occurs as the result of reading a book or two. Reading every book in the library will not guarantee the reader an educated imagination. The development of literacy and the education of the imagination through literature is a cumulative process resulting from a systematic and progressive study of literature. And the early study of literature must take its place in a continuum of study if the cumulative benefits of a literary education are to be realized.

The Need for Theory

Literature is widely considered to be primarily useful in supplying children with the sociological and psychological insights they need to interpret the world and survive in it. It is seen as a useful supplement to and aid in other learning such as social studies and science. The teaching of reading and the teaching of literature are generally regarded as entirely separate issues. The former is considered the proper major concern of the elementary school with literature functioning to stimulate interest in reading or to provide material for the practice of reading skills.

It is widely believed that significant literary study is beyond the scope of younger students. The study of literature as an art, apparently conceived of as something onerous and pedantic, is held suspect by many who fear that the child's sense of wonder and delight in story and poetry are jeopardized if he is asked to consider his literary experiences as anything more than diversion.

This curious viewpoint suggests that study, like medicine, must be unpleasant to be effective. Even those who believe that the benefits of teaching literature are too important for it to be approached in a haphazard and unsystematic fashion are wary of teaching literature in the elementary school. Their unwillingness may be an indictment of their own educational experience in classrooms where the study of poems was really verse vivesection and the reading of a story signaled the assignment of a page of questions to be answered for homework. Their ambivalence may well be caused by problems of definition and interpretation.

What it means to "study literature" has long been an open question, not only in the elementary school but in high schools and colleges as well. There are almost as many approaches to the subject as there are teachers of it. Literature curricula are characteristically planned in *ad hoc* fashion: built around themes like survival or courage, developed chronologically, set up by periods or countries, or incorporated with other studies in the humanities. Although such approaches may have some validity, they are essentially piecemeal and haphazard and give students little sense of the unity of the study with a consequent loss of its impact.

The question of how literature should be taught to young children gives rise to more questions than answers. As one researcher put it:

> There is interest in the subject, but there are more questions than answers about objectives, content, and approaches for teaching literature in kindergarten through grade six. . . . The expression "teaching literature" is used relatively infrequently. . . . The broader, more general interpretations of literature in the elementary school expand into use of terms such as language, language arts, personal reading, individualized reading, interests and tastes, reading guidance, literature readers, appreciation, and variations of these.*

The fundamental concepts on which the study of literature might be based and upon which more advanced studies can later be built have not been given adequate consideration. The teaching of literature suffers in comparison with science and mathematics from not having more theory of this kind—it is possible to educate the imagination as systematically as mathematics and science train the reason. It is as easy, if not easier, for a child to learn the mean-

*Norine Odland, *Teaching Literature in the Elementary School* (Urbana, Ill.: National Council of Teachers of English, 1969), p. 1.

ing of rhythm, plot, or form as it is to learn the meaning of sets, area, or equivalent fractions.

It is time to abandon the *ad hoc* approach to this important area of study. There is no legitimate excuse for delaying significant instruction until a child comes of high school age. Young children are perfectly capable of genuine intellectual activity if it is tailored to their needs, interests, and level of intellectual achievement.

Children's literature must cast off its Cinderella rags. For too long it has been a servant in the classroom: used to teach reading skills, inculcate moral values, develop positive self-concepts, and/or provide insights into the history of other people and other lands. Of course it is true that literature is useful in doing all of these things and more. But literature is first of all an art and should be taught *as literature* for its own sake and for its own inherent values. Everything else associated with its study is of secondary consideration.

What "Teaching Literature" Means

It is convenient to say that we teach literature. But literary works cannot be directly "taught" or "learned"; they are *experienced*. The experience of literature is not directly transmittable from one to another. But the knowledge of what literature is and how it works *can* be taught.

What we teach and learn when we "study literature" is criticism—all the verbal trappings used to talk about it. This does not mean that the study of literature is merely an indirect learning *about* literary works. The experiencing of poems and stories is obviously of primary importance, but it is not something that can be taught. Every individual has his own private and personal reaction to a work. It may excite, inspire, and delight him, but experience alone does not build up his knowledge of what literature is all about. Experiencing a city full of buildings is not studying architecture. Experiencing works of literature as discrete entities does not add to one's knowledge of literature as a whole, and gives no sense of the coherence of the subject.

There needs to be created, through criticism, a sense of the progressive and systematic, an awareness of the significance of literature that goes beyond the experiencing of individual works. Criticism is an approach to literature that gives shape and structure to experience: it is not esoteric; it should not conjure up pictures of scholars in ivory towers writing articles for learned journals.

It is what happens anywhere literature is treated as an art.

Criticism begins in the experiencing of literature in all its forms, when, for instance, kindergarten children listen to a story or poem, delighting in it as an artistic entity. The process involves the child's learning to make a distinction between imaginative verbal structures and passages of factual discourse. It includes his learning to react to *the total structure* of a story or poem without necessarily trying to extract from it a Timeless Truth or Key Idea.

Comprehension of story content and form is part of criticism, with an emphasis on the affective and imaginative as well as on the cognitive aspects of comprehending. The teacher helps pupils grow in their ability to take in stories and poems as imaginative verbal constructs by asking questions specifically designed to foster literary understandings. Such questions are those that focus the child's attention on the elements of story as they interact in the shaping and structuring of the form of the literary work as a whole and not in bits and pieces of its content. They are questions that center, for example, not so much on what a character did and when he did it but on *why* he had to behave as he did to make his story happen.

The child's response to the literature he encounters is a central aspect of criticism. The response may come in the form of question or comment; it may involve sharing a favorite poem or retelling a familiar story; it may be an original composition in words, a drawing, a dramatization, a puppet play, a dance drama, or the story board for a film. In the attempt to guide and foster the child's growth in comprehension and responsiveness, a teacher guides responses, providing assistance in planning and structuring them, and opportunities for developing, sharing, and evaluating them.

Criticism includes comprehension of individual literary works considered *as* literature and the child's response to the work, but it does not end there. It continues with efforts to help the child unify and integrate all of his literary experiences, in and out of school, and gain a sense of the significance this art has for him.

Northrop Frye, the distinguished literary critic and an eminent professor at the University of Toronto, describes literature as the range of articulate human imagination from its heights to its depths, man's revelation to man. Criticism must lead to an awareness of the significance of that revelation. Students should eventually see that every work is part of this total structure or order of words created by the power of imagination. They should see, too, how literature is related to other works of the imagination.

It is this last component of criticism that provides for elementary literary criticism its place of significance in the continuum of literary studies. Children, with materials and methods appropriate to their level of maturity, can make a beginning in significant literary criticism. As they proceed through the levels of formal education, the basic understandings they have acquired will provide a foundation upon which more sophisticated understandings may be built. Through their consideration of the structural principles of literature, children are provided with a broader conception of what literature is. They are less likely, when they can fit isolated literary experiences into a pattern, to leave school thinking of literature as a collection of unrelated works, only some of which they enjoyed or remember, or regarding the study of literature as without application to their experiences out of school.

The study of literature—criticism—begins in the kindergarten and continues through graduate school. The aim of the study is not to develop professional reviewers, scholars, or researchers. The aim is more fully developed human beings. Genuine criticism is a systematic study that treats literature as an art. It involves talking about literature in a way that will build up a systematic structure of knowledge *of* literature, taking the student beyond the subjectivity of his experience out into a wider, more comprehensive world.

Value Judgments

Direct experience of literature is highly personal and subjective and is more likely to end with a value judgment than a literary judgment. Value judgments made about literature invariably reveal more of the evaluator than the work. They are generally statements about the immediate effect of a poem or story on a reader. Value judgments are subjective evaluations, reflecting a given individual's personality, experience, and predilections.

Questions to children about what they like or dislike are not only futile in the critical sense but likely to be inhibiting. Refinements of taste, desirable though they may be, result from prolonged experience with the widest possible variety of the art, and they cannot be taught by or caught from another except in the most superficial sense. The teacher who attempts "to teach good taste" does so at the risk of alienating young readers who, at a particular moment in their lives, may find Nancy Drew or the Hardy Boys the nonpareil of literary form. Their personal response, redeemed by honesty, should, like grief, be private and respected. They should not be placed in the position of having to admit what it is they most enjoy or abhor, since this is not what constitutes a genuine criticism of literature. What one likes, in any case, is often what one has experienced; the new or unusual is likely to be suspect. The skilled teacher provides opportunities for broadening experience by introducing and making palatable and interesting a wide range of material and providing unlimited choice to satisfy a variety of tastes and preferences. The teacher's responsibility in matters of taste and judgment lies entirely with his ability to interest children in literature *of all kinds*. One of his finest qualities is his ability to refrain from expressing dismay at the personal preferences of the inexperienced. The teacher understands that the ability to evaluate is a by-product of genuine criticism and not its primary objective.

Genuine criticism is centered in knowledge rather than value judgments. It is more comparative than evaluative. It involves an effort by the student of literature to examine and interpret each work in terms of all the literature he knows.

Unifying Function of Criticism

Genuine criticism demonstrates that literature is a coherent order. It shows how each literary work is a part of that order and how nonliterary imaginative structures like advertisements, commercials, and popular songs are related to it. To accomplish this, criticism must be founded on a theory that defines the structural principles of literature. Without such theory criticism remains merely commentary, informed or otherwise, that seldom shows how literary works are fundamentally related.

Without a sense of structure it is impossible to see how things are related. Without an understanding of the structure of literature as a whole it is impossible to see how each separate work of literature relates to the whole.

Northrop Frye was the first to attempt a delineation of the structural principles of literature. He has provided a scheme that allows us to see all the phenomena literary criticism deals with as parts of a whole. His literary theory, set out in its most complete form in his *Anatomy of Criticism*, provides the means for a new approach to the study of literature at all levels. In the next two chapters this theory is interpreted and related specifically to children's literature. Professor Frye has seen the fundamental unity in literature. Literature as a whole he calls "one story," the quest myth: the quest of the human imagination for identity. The framework of all literature is a myth or archetypal story that goes like this: Once man lived in a paradisal garden or golden age in harmony with the universe. Man lost his perfect home, became alienated from nature and other men, and subject to time and death. The quest to recover the lost golden age is man's attempt to regain his human identity. It is the same goal sought by him as he tries to turn his environment into a human home.

The quest myth is central to all literature and suggests the critic's social function. If this central myth envisions the fulfillment of human desires, the establishment of the totally human society, criticism is the activity that can unite literature with society. This is done by interpreting and systematizing the vision of the artist and making it accessible to all, a humanistic study of immense importance.

Criticism, properly undertaken, is a study of how imagination works in the creation of art in words. In the process, the student's own imagination is developed and his capacity for vision enlarged. Criticism, properly undertaken, leads to a conception of literature as a coherent structure. With this conception comes awareness of its significance in one's own life, and in the lives of all.

Chapter 3

The Structural Principles
of Literature

Literature is more than a collection of unrelated poems and stories; the more we read the more obvious this becomes. Hercules and Superman were created centuries apart but they are recognizable as the same character type: the hero with magical powers. We find images like gardens and wastelands in the Old Testament and in the songs of Bob Dylan and Pete Seeger. That love is more powerful than any evil or even death itself is a theme found in stories as different as "Beauty and the Beast" and *Charlotte's Web.* We recognize the shape of the romance story in ancient epics and in today's westerns. The "good" cowboy, remarkably like the knightly hero of old, goes forth with faithful horse and trusty weapon on a quest to rid the world of evil.

The recurring structural patterns of literature—characters, images, themes, story shapes, events, and symbols—are *archetypes.* They are fundamental patterns that occur again and again in the literature of all ages. Nor are these units of imaginative thought common only to the main body of literature, they turn up in comics and films, in advertisements, in the writings of children. The archetype of the establishment of a "rightful kingdom" we can find in such different places as John F. Kennedy's Inaugural Address, in the Greek myth of Perseus, and in the song "Aquarius" from the musical *Hair.* The idealized green and golden world of romance is a favorite archetype of advertisers, for who can resist a product when it is associated with beauty, youth, and good times in a world of forever-summer?

17

Archetypes are intuitive, timeless, and stable. In them are expressed all our basic human concerns: who we are, where we come from, where we are going, how we should live. They are the concepts that give literature its unity.

The word *convention* expresses another kind of similarity we find in literature. If we read a detective story, for instance, we expect to find certain elements in it—a crime, someone to solve it, a criminal who is apprehended. Each detective story, like each game of chess or checkers, is different enough from others to make it a distinct experience, yet similar enough to make us recognize it as one of a type. In addition, we find that literary works fall into categories or genres. We expect a comedy to have certain features that a tragedy will not have. Comedies, in general, turn "up" at the end; tragedies turn "down."

The content of each story is unique, just as each infant is a unique human being. But, just as a baby is recognizably a member of the human race, stories are recognized by the various recurrent patterns within them as members of the whole family of literature. Literature grows out of other literature, deriving its forms from itself. And every form or pattern in literature has a pedigree. We can trace its descent back to the earliest times.

Literary Patterns from Mythology

From its beginnings literature has been man's imaginative attempt to give shape, order, and structure to his experience. It began with myth and ritual, the myth being the spoken part of a ritual, the story that the ritual enacts. Early religious rituals aimed at securing the well-being of a people and all shared the same general pattern: they depicted the death and resurrection of a god-king in a series of episodes that typically included a battle in which the god-king was victorious, a triumphal procession, an enthronement, a ceremony to ensure the destinies of the people for the coming year, and a sacred marriage.

Confronted with an alien universe, man, the storytelling animal, described natural phenomena in human terms. Occurrences in nature that frightened and bewildered him were given human shapes and "controlled" through story by means of analogy and metaphor. The clearest forms of such associations are in mythical images where we have "gods" who are human in shape and character, yet identified with something in nature like the sun or the seasons. The successful completion of a god-king's ritual quest signified human control over the natural world.

Feeling lost and helpless against the forces of nature, early man told stories of a time when he and nature were in harmony. The story of the Garden of Eden is one such story but similar ones are to be found in the mythology of many cultures. The story tells how man lost his perfect home, became alienated from the rest of the universe, and subject to time and death. By the power of his imagination man seeks to regain the lost perfect world. In later stories—legends and folk tales—the gods take on more human characteristics and have less divine power. Eventually they disappear from stories and characters become more and more recognizable as limited human beings. Even so, there always exists the desire, expressed in poems, stories, and even in the lyrics of a popular song, to "get back to the garden." Our literature is a continuous journal of man's search for identity, a metaphorical quest to rediscover a lost perfection. In modern literature nature is no longer a threat, but the world often seems an alien place, and stories still tell of the individual's efforts to find a place in it.

For constructing any work of art you need some principle of repetition or recurrence, like rhythm in music and pattern in painting. In the early development of literature from myth, the storyteller took for his recurring pattern the cycles of nature and eventually made analogies between the natural cycles and the human life cycle.

Mythologies are filled with tales of young gods or heroes—Perseus, Theseus, Hercules—who go through various successful adventures, endure great dangers, are deserted, betrayed, even killed, but who usually emerge safely in the end. The movement of the stories is analogous to the progression of the seasons or of the sun across the sky. The merging of the natural cycle with mythology provided myths with two opposing movements: the rising movement that we find in myths of birth, marriage, and resurrection; and the falling movement in myths of death, metamorphosis, or sacrifice. Later these movements appear as the rising movement of comedy and the falling movement of tragedy.

These early stories reveal another aspect of man's imagination. The hero's quest also involves a dialectical or philosophical way of looking at life, reflecting at one limit what man most desires and at the other what he most hates and fears. Myths project a paradise above the world of experience, a place of wish-fulfillment in which all obstacles are overcome. Below it, they project a hell, a world of nightmare and bondage. To the quest for identity, then, is added this goal: the possession of a state where man is released from an indifferent world into the upper world of his dreams, a world that is the opposite of his nightmares. These two opposing worlds appear in literature as the idealized world of romance and the absurd, suffering, frustrated world of irony and satire (as illustrated in the figure on the facing page).

Out of the cycle of death and renewal and man's emotional response to it there gradually emerged the four fundamental themes of imaginative experience: 1) romance, 2) tragedy, 3) comedy, 4) irony-satire. In romance we see how strong and beautiful heroes and heroines set out in search of the ideal green and golden world, the world of forever-summer. Tragedy tells how man, although he is capable of great things, has limited powers. He is sometimes a victim of forces he doesn't understand and cannot control. Just as the autumn leaves must fall so he must inevitably move toward his death. Irony and satire present the wintry world of experience where life is often as harsh and cruel as the winter winds. In comedy we find hopeful stories of the renewal of the human spirit. New life springs up as new growth comes again in the spring. Just as the seasons may be considered as distinct though related, so the four imaginative patterns may be seen as parts of the "one story," man's collective imaginative efforts to give shape to all of human experience.

John Keats's "The Human Seasons" is only one of many literary examples showing how "the mind of man" relates nature's cycles to his own life:

Four seasons fill the measure of the year;
    There are four seasons in the mind of man:
He has his lusty Spring, when fancy clear
    Takes in all beauty with an easy span:
He has his Summer, when luxuriously
    Spring's honied cud of youthful thought he loves
To ruminate, and by such dreaming high
    Is nearest unto heaven: quiet coves
His soul has in its Autumn, when his wings
    He furleth close; contented so to look
On mists in idleness—to let fair things
    Pass by unheeded as a threshold brook.
His has his Winter too of pale misfeature,
Or else he would forego his mortal nature.

These two thought constructs (the cycle, together with the image of an upper ideal world and its opposite) underlie all of literature. Even a brief lyric poem, although it does not tell a "story,"

Literary Imagery

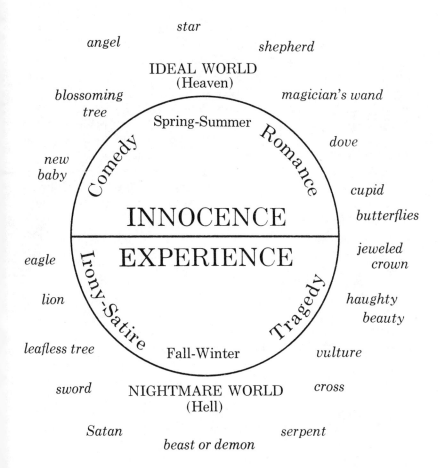

may express the emotions connected with the comic, spring part of the cycle or those related to the wintry world of irony. Because it is so structured, literature is in itself a coherent unity. Within this essentially simple structure one can fit all one's literary experiences. Each poem and story takes on a greater significance for it may be seen as part of a whole. The whole is the art of literature, man's imaginative attempt to make sense of the world and his existence in it.

The literature of every culture is shaped by its mythology. The Bible and classical mythology supply Western literature with the structure that informs it. The Old and New Testaments of the Bible together provide us with the most complete form we have of the archetypal story of the loss and recovery of identity, the story that is the framework of our literature. The Old Testament begins with the story of the creation of man (Adam) in paradise, then goes on to tell of his fall from innocence and the loss of his original home. Eventually the story of Adam becomes the story of Israel, a people who endure a long exile in a wilderness where they cannot feel at home, and who quest to reestablish the ideal world—the rightful kingdom—they once knew here on earth. The New Testament tells of the coming of the second Adam (Christ), who rescues the human race from the wilderness and restores the lost paradise where man is at one with himself and God. The classical myths give us more clearly than does the Bible the main episode of the central myth of the hero whose mysterious birth, triumph, betrayal, death, and rebirth follow the rhythm of the seasons. All stories in literature are developments of fundamental shapes that are seen most clearly in myths, particularly the myth that tells of the quest of the hero.

Our literature is actually a series of "displacements" from the level of pure myth (religion) to naturalism or realism, the mode of most serious fiction in Western literature for the past hundred years. (Literature for children, until recently comic or romantic, is now increasingly being written in the realistic mode.) The images, themes, characters, and plots are "displaced" to make them rationally credible and acceptable to a particular audience, a point that becomes clear when we consider literature both historically and in terms of the principal character's powers of action.

At the level of pure myth we have characters who are divine, supernatural figures superior to men and nature. Next come the heroes of epics who are superior in degree to other men and to their environments, moving in a world where the ordinary laws of nature are suspended, and often in close touch with the gods themselves. The next level features princes, kings, and noblemen who are portrayed as superior to other men but not to their environment. At the next remove, the hero has powers similar to our own. The farthest displacement from myth is the ironic-satiric mode where we find the anti-hero who is inferior in power even to ordinary men, a victim of others and the powers of nature.

Cyclical and Dialectical Imagery

The archetypal structures that underlie literary imagery are of two kinds: cyclical (imagery based on natural cycles) and dialectical (images that present contrasting worlds). Over and over in literature, images of the cycles of nature recur. Countless stories involve a cyclical journey, the hero or heroine returning in the end to the point of departure after a quest is completed. The pattern of the cyclical journey is common to tales old and new: Odysseus's story shows it, as does *The Tale of Peter Rabbit* and modern fantasies like *Where the Wild Things Are.*

Often associations are made between human and animal life and the daily or seasonal cycles. The rejected Ugly Duckling suffers his greatest loneliness in the winter when the ground is frozen and barren. He finds his identity in the springtime in a garden where apple trees are in bloom and the scent of lilac is in the air. When the Norse god Balder lies dead in Asgard, darkness spreads over heaven and earth, the "night of death." Johnny Appleseed dies but he is memorialized each spring when the apple trees bloom. In Robert Frost's "Stopping by Woods on a Winter Evening" the temptation to give up is associated with winter and the darkest evening of the year. In "Old Man and the Beginning of the World," a myth of the Blackfeet Indians, Old Man promises to return like the sun as he disappears into the west. In more westerns than we can count, the hero rides off into the sunset, not to die but to be reborn in yet another episode of his endless story. The epic hero Gilgamesh, in his quest to find the secret of life and death, follows the "way of the sun" to the Eastern Garden, the sun's dwelling.

Spring and summer are associated frequently with new beginnings, with joy and hope, youth and the prime of life. Autumn and winter are as often associated with old age, death, decay, and loss.

Above and below the world of man's experience, myth projects an upper, desirable ideal world (the heaven of religion) and its opposite, an undesirable nightmare state (hell). The main body of literature is not religious, however, and does not deal with heaven and hell. The human experience is seen as analogous to these contrasting worlds. William Blake called these human worlds *innocence* and *experience*. The imagery of the heavenly world reaches down into the world of innocence; that of the demonic, up into the world of experience. (See sketch on page 21.) The heavenly world gives us images of gods like Zeus and the Oympians, a sky-father like Odin, the three-in-one god of the Christian religion. The demonic world is peopled with malicious gods like Satan, revealed through images of menacing natural forces like the sea in Armstrong Sperry's *Call It Courage,* or is represented by a blind fate against which man has no defenses. The tragic deaths of young innocents like Nadia in Jaap Ter Haar's *Boris* and Raidy in *The Loner* by Ester Weir are examples of imagery of the latter type.

The innocent world is one of romance, or of stories and poems with a comic or upward movement. Here good parents, wise old men, and benevolent fairy godmothers are analogous to the divinities of the heavenly world; false fathers, wicked stepmothers, and ambitious kings, to the undesirable gods of the demonic world. King Arthur's mentor, Merlin, and Chiron, instructor of Greek heroes like Achilles and Jason, are good examples of the wise old men who counsel the young. The cruel stepmother of "Snow White" and the vicious witch who captures Hansel and Gretel are typical of the heartless hags and other varieties of horrible women whose images haunt the tragic, ironic, sad visions of life. In a modern story, Julia Cunningham's *Dorp Dead,* the evil Kobalt is a literary relative once-removed from the wicked sorcerers and wizards of old fairy tales who are themselves one step away from the gods of the underworld. The hunter in the same book who befriends young Gilly provides an opposite image: that of counselor and benefactor. The story takes place in the human sphere but in the character of the hunter is an image that resembles the benevolent deity of the heavenly world.

Sky images come "down" and "up" from the heavenly and demonic worlds into the literary worlds that deal with human concerns. It becomes clear that knowledge of biblical and classical imagery will make the reading of all subsequent literature more richly meaningful. In the heavenly sphere we have the sun and the angels, the thunder of Zeus, and Prometheus's gift of the gods' fire to man. At the opposite pole is Lucifer and images of fire and brimstone. In between the world of fire may be one of malignant demons like the will-o'-the-wisp in tales old and new. In the innocent world fire is usually a purifying symbol, a world of flame that none but the pure may pass through. Sigurd, alone of all the Volsungs, is able to penetrate the wall of fire that surrounds Brynhild. In the story of the Sleeping Beauty the wall of fire is replaced by one of thorns and brambles, but the images are closely related. In the world of experience the heavenly fire blazes in the jewels of the king's crown and the flashing eyes of the beautiful lady.

Human images in the heavenly world are those of mankind as members of one body, united in God. At the beginning of the eighth book of the Iliad, Zeus remarks that, should he desire to do so, he can pull up the whole chain of being, both gods and humans, into himself, the supreme divine will. There are images of the Good Shepherd, pastor of a human flock. In the demonic world the human images indicate disorder and ruthlessness. Among them are cruel tyrants who demand human sacrifices, bloodthirsty mobs, and sirens like those in the Odyssey who tempt men to forget their humanity. In the world of innocence that we see in romance, kings and lords abound, analogous to the gods of heaven. Here the peasant and commoner are idealized, with poor but worthy lads like Boots meeting success against all odds.

In more "realistic" stories in the world of experience there is more relationship in imagery to the demonic world. Order and reason and justice do not prevail as in the innocent worlds of comedy and romance. Characters are common and typical men and women subject to all the ills that beset mankind. Here characters are more likely to be victims than triumphant heroes. The boy and his family in William Armstrong's *Sounder*, the young escapee from the concentration camp in Anne Holm's *North to Freedom*, and the lonely young orphan in Ester Weir's *The Loner* are examples.

Animal imagery in the innocent world strongly reflects the biblical and classical. Domesticated animals, notably the sheep, are symbols of devotion and loyalty, analogous to the Lamb of God. The dove and other gentle birds provide images of peace and love. Unicorns and dolphins contrast with the dragons and monsters of the demonic world. In the Bible we have the monster Leviathan, symbolic of the whole fallen world of sin, tyranny, and death in which man lives. Traditional tales like those of St. George and Beowulf commonly show the heroes fighting evil in the form of dragons and monsters.

Vegetable imagery in the heavenly world is well known to us. Both the Bible and classical mythology tell of gardens of paradise. The tree of life contrasts with the demonic cross. In the human worlds of innocence and experience, enchanted gardens and beautiful parks are just once removed from heavenly gardens. In romance pastoral settings like Sherwood Forest are desirable images. Many modern realistic stories with harsh, bleak urban settings show by contrast that the rural setting is still seen as closer to man's vision of the ideal. A romantic counterpart to the tree of life appears in the wand of the magician and the fairy godmother, which can provide life and miraculous change.

Demonic imagery is lacking entirely in lush vegetation. Hell is a rocky wasteland where no trees and plants grow. Its counterpart in modern stories of human experience is the concrete and glass city, often depicted as a place of alienation and despair, as in Paula Fox's *How Many Miles to Babylon* and Mary Weik's *The Jazz Man.*

In the Bible we have images of temples and jeweled cities paved with gold. These are reflected in the enchanted castles, courts, and capital cities of romance, and are frequently the goal of young travelers who journey on the highroad in search of treasure or a better life. The highroad itself may be seen as the counterpart of "the one way" of biblical imagery.

Water imagery extends all the way from the water of life to the Deluge. In romance literature the hero often descends into or under water just as the soul of biblical imagery sinks into it at death. For the hero of romance a descent into water may be a kind of ritual death. Mafatu in Armstrong Sperry's *Call It Courage* emerges from submersion in the sea reborn with a new identity. Water in the world of innocence may be symbolic of growth and fertility or seen, like the biblical ritual of baptism, as a purifier. King Midas must bathe himself in a pool to remove the stigma of the golden touch.

Dominic by William Steig shows how a contemporary writer for children makes use of conventional imagery. The hero is Dominic, a cheerful, gregarious mutt who leaves home to seek his fortune, to find adventure and a more satisfying life. Along the way he encounters his adversaries, the evil Doomsday Gang: foxes, weasels, ferrets, a wildcat, a wolf, tomcats, dingoes, and rats. The hero and those he befriends in the course of his travels are gentler animals, friendly to man and not given to preying on each other. Another friend is the helpful and wise woman in the form of an alligator witch. She shares her magic powers with him by giving him her wand in the shape of a sword that will make him invincible in combat.

Dominic sets out upon his adventures along a springtime road strewn with leafy trees and flowers. In the story the forest is the setting for the hero's greatest trials, confusion, and despair. It is only with great difficulty that Dominic is able to "get out of the woods" to safety. He finds treasure both in the form of diamonds, rubies, and emeralds and in someone to love. His love he discovers in a miniature palace in a beautiful enchanted garden where it is always summer. His dreams of a new and more fulfilling life have come ture.

An examination of poetry written by children indicates that they have an intuitive grasp of these basic patterns of poetic image-ry. Just as their first grasp of these patterns in what they read and hear is intuitive, so it is when they write to order their feelings and impressions. The following poems are all taken from *Poetic Composition Through the Grades* by Robert A. Wolsch. In the first example loneliness is associated with the cold wind of autumn:

> Child lonely playing
> In the cold and growling wind
> Sees a lone leaf drift.

In another, a child expresses a happy wish of flying high to a dance in the sky:

> If I could fly
> I'd roar through the sky
> So high! So high!! So high!!!
> I'd do all kinds of tricks
> I would! I would!
> I'd dance in the sky with all the birds,
> And when the day is over
> I'd rest on a silver white cloud.
> Wouldn't you
> Do that too?
> If you
> Could fly?!
> Fly!!!!!

The happy freedom of the flying bird contrasts with the sadness of the earthbound boy who is cheered by the bird who joins him to walk "on the dirt road" that is the boy's natural home:

> A beautiful bird
>   flew in the sky
>   and
> A sad little boy
>   sitting in the sand.
>   then

> The beautiful bird
> flew on his shoulder
>   and
> sang to him
>   and
> the sad little boy
> happy again
>   and
> they both walk
> on the dirt road.

Natural phenomena are seen as predatory animals:

> The darkening clouds,
> Blot out the sky,
> Thunder roaring like hungry tigers,
> Searching for their prey.
>   . . .

A conscious knowledge of the archetypal patterns of imagery will bring shape and focus to the child's own writing. Discussion of the symbols and images he will use to express ideas, wishes, dreams, nightmares, and the like will inform his own writing and enlighten his appreciation and understanding of the writing of others.

Taken together, the patterns of imagery and the narrative plots give us a structural framework within which all literary works will be found to have a place. This is not to say that every poem, play, and story should be prodded and pared until it fits into a slot. The framework simply provides us with an *organizational scheme* that enables us to see literature as a whole rather than as a collection of unrelated entities. Seeing literature as a whole allows us to feel its full imaginative impact and to recognize the ultimate power of the human imagination. This awareness should come to the student through a process of discovery. It will do no good to *tell* young students what the structural patterns of literature are. They must find them out for themselves. The framework is for teachers to use when structuring learning experiences designed to bring students to these basic understandings.

Chapter 4

The Four Plots

The content of each story we read in a book or watch on a screen may be different: the possible combinations of characters and incidents are infinite. What is limited is the number of ways in which stories may be told. Northrop Frye has described four basic story forms or plots that remain constant as the constructive principles used to shape story content; his description is the referent for this chapter.

The four "stories" or plots form a ring or circle of stories (as illustrated by the drawing that appears on the next page). They merge into one another at their limits. Where they overlap we have romantic comedies, for instance, or ironic tragedies. Within each basic plot are variations of it.

The framework is exemplified in the basic story of the quest of the hero. The circle of stories starts with romance, which develops out of the mythical story of the hero's adventures. His sufferings and trials, his brushes with death, are the focal points of tragedy and irony-satire. The circle ends with comedy, which develops out of the hero's triumph in his successful quest. Taken together, the four basic stories provide an imaginative shape for each aspect of the human experience. No one story is the whole story. All of the stories together are part of the one story: man's quest for his human identity.

The Circle of Stories

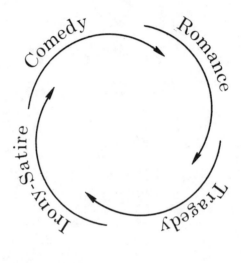

The First Story: Romance

The romance story is one of the great narrative patterns devised by the imagination, a form in which wishes come true,
goodness always triumphs over evil, where heroes and heroines
"live happily ever after" in peace and plenty. Although there are
variations within the romance form, the basic quest is a cyclical
pattern involving three principal stages: a dangerous or marvelous
journey; a central struggle, test, or ordeal; and a return to the point
from which the journey began. This complete form is most clearly
seen in the stories of the epic heroes: Perseus, Theseus, Sigurd,
Beowulf, Odysseus.

Other stories, actually episodes within the romance form, may
tell of the birth of the hero and his early days. His birth, like that
of Moses, is often shrouded in mystery and secrecy. His early life
yields stories of extraordinary powers: Paul Bunyan wields his axe
in babyhood, Hercules is still an infant when he strangles the ser-
pents sent by Hera to kill him. There may be false "fathers" or

"mothers" who seek the child's death; Pharaoh, Herod, and the wicked stepmothers of folk tales are examples. Often the child is prepared for the illustrious life he will lead by kindly foster parents or wise teachers like Merlin in the story of King Arthur.

There are stories of innocence pressing toward experience; an example is Joseph Krumgold's . . . *and now Miguel.* In other romance stories, the power of innocence overcomes evil or ugliness, as in "Beauty and the Beast" or "Soldier Jack."

Since romance is a wish-fulfillment dream it may also, in some of its forms, show the shadow side of romance: the world we most want to avoid. Here fantasy descends to horror, the hero doing battle with horrible monsters and giants, perhaps even with Death himself. Romance literature in its demonic vein contains the sinister and horrible images associated with nightmares. There are tales of the supernatural, or of magic powers that operate on the side of evil. Frankenstein's creation is like the scary giants and ogres of fairy tales, a dream turned into a nightmare.

On its simplest level the quest is a search for adventure. But, because of its association with the good and the ideal, the quest always has a deeper significance. It is more than adventure for its own sake. The object of the quest determines the seriousness of the tone. Beowulf goes to slay a monster who is laying waste a kingdom; Theseus, to kill the minotaur and put an end to tyranny; Perseus, to destroy the Gorgon Medusa whose terrifying visage turns all who look upon her to stone. Countless sons in folk tales go off to seek their fortunes. The quester may be rewarded with something tangible: a treasure, a bride, lands, or a kingdom. He may gain wisdom or magic powers. Symbolically the quest means more. It represents a journey into the darker parts of human nature where the hero confronts evil and even death itself in his efforts to discover his relationship to nature, to other men, to his own self. Whatever tangible treasures may result from the quest, perhaps the greatest benefit is the hero's discovery of himself and his powers. In its deepest sense it seems to be a search for the knowledge of what it means to be human, of what is involved in taking one's place in the pattern of human civilization as a fully functioning member of society.

The hero's quest may be compared to the rites of passage rituals of primitive tribes. Typically the initiate is isolated from his people, given instruction, and made to undergo some ordeal to test his strength or wit. When he has survived the ordeal he is reunited with the tribe amid feasting and rejoicing. He may be given a new name to symbolize his rebirth as a mature member of the society.

The myth of the hero is common to all civilizations, from the ancient Babylonians to contemporary primitive tribes. Its ubiquity suggests that the pattern of romance—the quest—embodies a fundamental pattern of human experience. It has an essential function in the development of the individual's awareness of his strengths and weaknesses, with psychological as well as ritual or tribal significance.

The two central characters of the romance are the hero who is symbolically associated with spring, dawn, youth, and vigor and his adversary who is associated with winter, darkness, old age, and sterility. The hero of romance is often described as being larger-than-life. He is larger not so much because he is superhuman (though he may possess extraordinary powers) but rather in the sense that he has a vision of a world that is more perfect than the one we live in and a belief in his ability to make that world a reality.

The romance hero is a highly idealized figure, usually embodying the virtues held noblest by the societies from which his stories came. He is strong and courteous, durable and self-controlled. He embodies highly civilized virtues like intelligence, wit, and above all, imagination and vision. Although he may not be a god or even the son of one, he has a mysterious contact with a world beyond the world of experience from which he seems to derive a power denied to ordinary mortals. He is a leader, someone at the frontiers of experience. His triumphs benefit all around, his powers lift others toward the heights he scales.

Typical romances move toward progress or fulfillment: victory, the acquisition of treasure, a better life. The achievement involves herculean efforts on the part of the hero, with or without help from others. In the end his life is transformed: he may be released from a threatening past, come to know himself, or be brought to some significant understanding. Most other characters in the romance are one-dimensional. They are either good or bad, for the hero or against him. Good women in romance are usually rescued maidens or brides or supporters of the hero; bad women are cast as evil stepmothers, witches, and temptresses. The people who inhabit the pages of romance are not particularly realistic. They are more like the desirable characters of our dreams and the undesirable characters of our nightmares.

The settings of romance are generally idyllic or at least removed from the world of ordinary experience. There are possibilities of magic and miracles. Things of nature, trees and animals, often have a mysterious rapport with the hero, coming to his aid. Birds warn Snow White of her danger; folk and fairy tales are full of talking animals who aid the hero. We find this in "The Flea," a Spanish folktale, and in the story of "Drakestail."

Visions and revelations are common to romance. In stories that deal with moral opposites it is not surprising that there be some means of connecting a "heavenly" world with a "lower" one. The union is frequently achieved by a vision or insight (in more modern romances) that takes place in a high or isolated place like a mountain top, an island, or a tower. Jacob's ladder is an example of this enjoinment of the two worlds.

The Tale of Peter Rabbit, durable and delightful, has been a source of literary satisfaction to generations of youngsters. It is a prime example of the well-constructed story, an example of the romance form in miniature. The hero faces a perilous journey with minor adventures, a crucial struggle, and final exaltation or success, the whole expressing the passage from a point of ritual death to the "resurrection" of the recognition scene.

Peter sets out in defiance of his mother to seek identity, an identity undoubtedly associated with his father who had met an untimely death in Mr. McGregor's garden. The young adventurer undergoes a series of hairsbreadth escapes. He loses his jacket and shoes, is wet and frightened, and escapes only after he finds himself a vantage point that gives him, together with his fleetness of foot, an advantage over his enemy. In the end, as a result of his own efforts, he is safely home, undoubtedly a proven hero, although he has lost his clothes, is not feeling well, and is put to bed with a dose of camomile tea. His well-behaved siblings have bread and milk and blackberries for supper, but it is Peter who is most emphatically the hero of the piece since he is the one who has successfully completed a quest.

The characterization in Peter Rabbit follows the typical conflict pattern of the romance. There are two main characters: Peter, the protagonist, and Mr. McGregor, the antagonist. At the lowest point of his trials, when he is imprisoned in the gooseberry net, Peter is encouraged by three friendly sparrows who "implored him to exert himself," characters with literary relatives among the children-of-nature figures common to romance, morally neutral and helpful to the hero. The very proper siblings are foils for Peter, emphasizing by their docility the enormity of Peter's ambition and daring. The comforting figure of Mrs. Rabbit waiting at home until the hero finishes his wanderings is similar to wife-mother figures in more ambitious and lengthier works: Solveig of *Peer Gynt*, for example, and Penelope in the *Odyssey*.

For older children, *Call It Courage* is another example of the romance plot. Mafatu, son of the great chief of a Polynesian tribe, lives in fear of the sea, for as a young child he came perilously close to drowning while his mother lost her life as she rescued him. He is reduced to women's work on the island, scorned by his peers as a coward, and a disappointment to his father. The reason for Mafatu's quest is clear—he must find his identity in a face-to-face battle with his enemy, the sea.

Mafatu sets out on his perilous journey, weathering a storm and the destruction of his canoe on a reef. Finally he reaches a desolate island where he sets to work to make a shelter and replacements for the canoe and the weapons he has lost. The sheltering island itself contains a threat, for it is the site of the holy place of sacrifice of a cannibal tribe who will surely return and seek to destroy Mafatu when they know he has desecrated their sacred ground. Yet he sets out calmly to build his boat, gaining courage with every action of his own hand. He kills a wild boar with a weapon of his own making, saves his dog from a tiger shark, and kills an octopus in a daring underwater fight. Drums announce the arrival of the cannibals, but Mafatu's boat is ready and he eludes his pursuers with skill and daring, and sails in the direction of home. He cries out triumphantly to the threatening sea that he no longer fears it, even when there seems little chance of his reaching home again. Mafatu at this moment has won his personal battle and regained his identity. It remains, however, for him to be exalted in the eyes of others and this happens when he lands safely home, a figure of mystery and magnificence.

In *Call It Courage* the sea is the antagonist, a personification of a being of unlimited strength, bent for revenge. Mafatu's only friends are misfits like himself: a nondescript yellow dog and a lame albatross. Like neutral nature spirits, they play a helping role: comforting the boy, giving him hope and companionship. And, in the case of Kivi the albatross, offering mysterious guidance as Mafatu begins his quest and ends it.

The romance form is popular in children's literature. It is found in picture storybooks like Maurice Sendak's *Where the Wild Things Are*, Edward Ardizzone's *Little Tim and the Brave Sea Captain*, Hardie Gramatky's *Little Toot*. The hero tales retold in language suitable for modern eyes and ears, particularly those written recently by Ian Serraillier and Roger Lancelyn Green, are superb examples of this form. William Steig's *Dominic* is, in structure, another fine specimen of the romance form.

Although it may appear with widely different subject matter

and expressing a variety of values, the romance plot or pattern has always been a favorite with children and those who write for them. Whether the romance is close to myth and magic like the old tales of heroes, a fantasy, or a realistic modern version of the form, there is no question about its power and importance in the development of the imagination. Romance tells of dreams and how they are made to come true. It deals in hope. It brings a message from the imagination to the imagination that every child will need if he is to slay his dragons.

The Second Story: Tragedy

Romance, as a story form, tells of wishes and dreams that come true. Poems and stories that explore the *limits* of man's power to make his wishes and dreams come true belong to the literary form we call tragedy. Destruction of the innocent, beautiful, or virtuous is something we feel should not happen. Yet such destruction is a fact of the human experience, no matter how unreasonable it may seem to us. Tragedy leaves us feeling helpless and vulnerable and reminds us that we are not all-powerful. Tragic stories often suggest that the hero is destroyed because he has broken some natural law or order, even though he may have done so in all innocence. They are imaginative attempts to balance man's potential greatness with his perishable nature, to come to terms with powers that are greater than his.

The central idea of tragedy is catastrophe or death befalling a heroic character. A tragedy may be romantic or ironic and realistic, depending on whether it features idealized or more realistic heroes and heroines. At the heroic extreme the tragic hero is given the greatest possible dignity, usually a product of his innocence and courage. Hans Christian Andersen's "Steadfast Tin Soldier" is such a hero, Balder of Norse mythology is another.

Another kind of heroic tragedy is the archetypal story of the loss of innocence, innocence being a lack of experience. Young people are baffled and defeated by their first contact with the adult world, as is Jane in Helen Fern Daringer's *Adopted Jane.* Such stories may tell of a youthful life cut off or of a child's first understanding of the significance of death.

Still another variation of the tragic story tells of the death, often a willing one, of the hero in support of some great cause. Beowulf deliberately gives his life to save his people. King Arthur knows that his whole life has been a sacrifice for a "dream of justice." This type of tragic story derives from the ancient ritual of the scapegoat: the evils of the tribe were ritualistically invested in an animal who was then driven into the wilderness to die. In the tragedy of sacrifice, the hero's society is purged of evil by his sacrifice, voluntarily made in their behalf.

The tragedy of sacrifice is a grave reminder of what it costs to be fully human in the noblest sense. The hero accepts fate and resists oppression at the cost of his life, his sacrifice saves those left behind. It is a sobering story but an exhilarating one, found in both epic tales like Beowulf and biographies of such men as Martin Luther King and Malcolm X.

Many tragic stories center around a character who is not of the world of innocence but of the world of experience. He is a puzzling character; he may be a great leader of men and in many respects heroic, but at the same time his character or outlook contains a flaw that leads him to make some disastrous mistake or choice. His action seems to provoke a situation that causes his inevitable downfall, a sense of his having disturbed the natural order. His story seems a kind of revenge, a hostile reaction from some power that is beyond him. Great classical tragedies like Antigone and King Lear are stories of this type.

As tragedy gets closer to irony in the circle of stories, heroes become more lifelike, no longer the larger-than-life figures just spoken of. Here are stories that reflect man's feeling of being caught in a trap from which he cannot free himself, of being a victim of vast and overwhelming forces that immobilize and imprison. In ironic literature we see man's spirit defeated under similar conditions. But in tragedy, even when all hope is lost, man retains his human dignity. By the very act of facing the realities and challenges of life, he overcomes them.

William Armstrong's *Sounder* shows us elements of this last type of tragic story. The father is a victim of circumstances beyond his control, a black sharecropper in Louisiana during the Depression. His opportunities are limited. Both nature and men are hostile. The land bears poor crops, and no one comes forward to help him feed his starving children; when he steals for them, his captors are ruthless in their punishment. Yet he endures through agonies of pain when the posse's guns injure him and through the knowledge of his family's suffering when he is taken off to prison. He returns home, body broken but spirit intact, to die with dignity, leaving that and his courage as a legacy of hope to his children.

Many children's stories have elements of tragedy in them but few are examples of the tragic form as we find it in adult literature.

Pigeon, Fly Home, a tragic story that deals with the destruction of a brave innocent, is no less tragic because the victim is a pigeon rather than a human being. Chad and his friends have a pigeon racing club, and he takes pity on the coffee-colored peeper that is the weakling of his flock. He tries to shelter it from the stronger pigeons who threaten to peck it to death, nurturing it against the advice of his fellow pigeon-fanciers who are able to view with more professional detachment the fate of weakling peepers.

Yet Chad is determined that his Leyden will not share the fate of the weak bird among the strong. He feeds her, protects her, and insulates himself from the jibes of less compassionate breeders. Eventually his pigeon comes into her own and is accepted by the flock.

Then, on her first flight, Leyden is attacked by a hawk. She returns home, safe but injured and unsteady, and is once again almost pecked to death by the others. Still Chad persists, though his efforts amount to perversity in the eyes of his less sentimental friends.

At last it seems that Chad's stubborn faith has been rewarded when Leyden becomes the best racer in the flock. Her early difficulties seem all in the past and Chad's hopes are high as he enters her in the big race of the season. She would have won, but at the height of her triumph she is attacked and brought down by two hawks. Hunters see her last gallant struggle and report how bravely she died.

Leyden's ability and final courage have won the admiration of the club members who once doubted her, and all of them share Chad's sense of helplessness and loss. But no one has words adequate to explain why Leyden's life was marked with tragedy.

The tragic story leaves us with a sense of wonder and awe. It raises questions men have never found answers for, fundamental questions about the ills that living creatures are subject to. Tragedy, as opposed to irony, does not leave us with a sense of hopelessness. The tragic figure may suffer, even die, but he characteristically displays the highest of human attributes: nobility and dignity.

The Third Story: Satire and Irony

Satire and irony are literary forms set in the world of experience, reflecting the discrepancy between what is and what ideally ought to be. Satire attempts to change man and society for the better, often by using bitter ridicule; irony details human limitations.

Both forms often parody the themes and archetypes of romance to make their points. The hero is not larger-than-life; he is all-too-human. He is subject to all the ills of the world: physical weakness, other man's inhumanity, his own neuroses. Time passes and he must grow old and die. There is no feeling, as there is in tragedy and romance, of mysterious powers that link the hero to something that transcends the world. Since he is merely man in a world that is far from ideal, his quests often remain unfulfilled or they are wrong-headed or without goals. The qualities of the hero—clear vision, endurance, ability—are absent. Or they are used by the hero-as-rogue who outwits the unscrupulous by becoming unscrupulous himself. The good and innocent are more likely to be victims than champions, and love is more often thwarted than conquering. The green world of romance is often replaced by the harsh concrete of the city slum.

In a sense the satirist is himself like the questing hero of romance. He chips away at the huge ills of humanity: hypocrisy, self-deceit, smugness, pettiness, injustice, but with little hope of curing them. In some satires people are shown accepting what they believe cannot be changed or retreating into rationalizations in an effort to escape it. There are stories granting that the world is full of crime and folly but counseling the reader to keep his balance, remember the tried and true, laugh at the follies around him and, in effect, accept the conventions of society.

Most satire is beyond the imaginative reach of young children and few authors write in this form for them. The satirical aspects of *Gulliver's Travels* and *Alice in Wonderland* are for the most part absorbed without notice as the story is enjoyed for its own sake. In Andersen's tales such as "The Ugly Duckling" and "The Emperor's New Clothes" children encounter the satire in a form more manageable by them. A number of recent books for young adolescents shows elements of satire: *Henry 3, Dinky Hocker Shoots Smack*, and *Freaky Friday* are some examples.

Ironic stories, like satiric ones, take place in the world of experience rather than in the world of innocence and with them, too, heroism is impossible. They differ from satire in that no moral ideal seems possible.

In recent years more and more children's literature has been written in the ironic mode of most contemporary adult literature. *The Pigman* by Paul Zindel, a story written for young adolescents, looks at tragedy from below, from the moral and realistic perspective of the state of experience. It stresses the humanity of its heroes, minimizes the sense of ritual inevitability found in tragedy, and supplies social and psychological explanations for catastrophe.

In *The Pigman* two precocious, perceptive, and lonely teenagers make friends with an equally lonely, strange old man, Mr. Pignati, who lives only through dreams of his dead wife and daily visits to his closest friend, a baboon at the zoo. The story is narrated alternately by the hero and heroine in a series of flashbacks, their attempt to make sense of all the crazy things they did. It is often funny in its digressions, wit, and candor, but the humor only serves to point up the irony that underlies it.

Alienated from their parents, John and Lorraine find the Pigman someone who accepts them as they are, spoils them a little, and genuinely enjoys their company, luxuries not to be found in their homes. Their zany relationship flourishes in love and laughter; they have the run of his cluttered old house, sharing with him food and trips to the zoo. He buys them gifts of roller skates and all three joyously skate down the hallway of his home. Human weakness and poor judgment are their undoing. Mr. Pignati suffers a heart attack after an hilarious skating session. While he is hospitalized, John and Lorraine invite friends to a party that turns his house into a shambles. His wife's collection of prized china pigs is smashed, her clothes ripped by the girls who dress up in them, and his belongings looted. In the midst of the chaos Mr. Pignati returns from the hospital. Although he forgives the stricken young people who are not sure how things got so far out of their control, his gay spirit is broken. When they persuade him the next day to take a trip to the zoo to see Bobo, his baboon friend, he agrees half-heartedly to go. Once there he discovers that Bobo has died while he was in the hospital. Mr. Pignati, weak from the heart attack, dies in front of the baboon cage.

John tries to sum up his feelings at the end, deploring life "in a world where you can grow old and be alone and have to get down on your hands and knees and beg for friends." He muses that maybe he and Lorraine for that matter are baboons, only of a different kind, and that his parents and everyone else are "baffled baboons concentrating on all the wrong things." The young people have faced reality and themselves, and found both confrontations unpleasant.

As structure, the central principle of ironic myth is best approached as a parody of romance. Simple though it is, "The Gingerbread Boy" is a good primer introduction to the ironic myth. The Gingerbread Boy, about to be eaten, escapes and rolls down the hill on a quest for freedom and safety, narrowly escaping all who would eat him, and that is everyone he meets, including the family from whom he first escaped. Freedom seems certain until the Gingerbread Boy makes a friend of Piggy Wiggy, who proves false. In the process of what seems a helpful act of carrying the Gingerbread Boy across a brook on his snout, the pig swallows him in one gulp. The Gingerbread Boy's quest is cut short unfulfilled.

Other stories in the ironic mode include John Neufeld's *Edgar Allen*, Eleanor Estes's *The Hundred Dresses*, Mary Weik's *The Jazz Man*, *Queenie Peavy* by Robert Burch, and *Adopted Jane* by Helen Fern Daringer.

Ironic stories reveal a very bitter picture of human existence: the contrast between ideals and reality. Today many people believe that children's literature must reflect life as it is and not see it through the rose-colored glasses of romance and comedy. There is some merit in this view, of course, but irony and satire do not present the whole story of man's experience any more than romance and comedy do. Irony, in fact, proves to be romance turned upside down, the nightmare instead of the dream. That they are the two sides of one coin is proof that we need them both. Implicit in the ironic story is the dream of how things "ought to be."

The Fourth Story: Comedy

When we speak of comedy, we are likely to think of laughter, but many forms of the comic plot in literature are not necessarily funny or humorous. They do, however, present a positive view of the human experience. Comedy is a form that celebrates the power of nature, human or otherwise, to renew itself, the power of life to overthrow the threat of death. It has to do with transformation, with the power of the imagination to raise experience above the limits of time and space, to change people and things into desirable images.

The central idea of comedy is rebirth or renewal after obstacles are overcome. The simplest pattern of comedy is expressed in the old cliché: boy meets girl, boy loses girl, boy and girl are reunited. The hero is kept from the object of his desires by a series of blocks or obstacles, often in the form of the intransigent adult. The comic form usually involves a movement from one kind of society to another: from the rule of impossible, unreasonable people to the establishment of a new society where everyone is happy.

This ending is achieved by almost any means at all: miraculous transformations, coincidences, magical interventions. But the audience is delighted even when the solution is most improbable, because they know that this is the only possible ending, that this is the way things ought to be. Even the intransigent characters are reformed and redeemed and become part of the new social order in the end. Scrooge in Dickens's *A Christmas Carol* is one of these.

The typical hero of comedy is like Wilbur in E. B. White's *Charlotte's Web*: likeable enough, but rather ordinary and conventional. He is aided by a cunning cohort, Charlotte, a character type common to comedy, one related to the "tricky slave" of ancient Roman comedies whose wit and daring frequently saved his charming but none-too-bright master. The chief blocking character is often a father figure, an outright villain, or is represented by an unfair or impossible situation that must be overcome, like the threat to Wilbur's life. Other comic characters include detractors of the hero, like Templeton the rat, and buffoons who contribute to the comic action with singing, clowning, and miscellaneous humor, like the gossipy goose in *Charlotte's Web*.

Like tragedies, comic plots may stretch from the limits of the ironic to the romantic. Julia Cunningham's *Dorp Dead* is an ironic comedy where the will to live triumphs over odds that must surely have left scars. *Charlotte's Web* and White's *The Trumpet of the Swan* are romantic comedies at the other end of the scale; from beginning to end the mood is one of hope.

An excellent example of the comic structure in children's literature is *The 500 Hats of Bartholomew Cubbins*, a comedy in the phase closest to romance. In this story there is a magical element that is never explained: the five hundred hats that appear successively on Bartholomew's head are a phenomenon that "just 'happened to happen' and was not very likely to happen again."

Bartholomew, much like the heroes of Dickensian comedy, is a likeable chap, unpretentious and brave enough when he must be. Through no fault of his own, he is confronted with a wrathful and unreasonable king who demands that Bartholomew remove his hat in his presence. The hero tries to comply but cannot—whenever he removes a hat, another appears in its place. Like the hero of a picaresque, a juvenile Tom Jones, he is whirled off into a series of adventures, more or less an innocent victim of circumstances and situations largely beyond his control.

The characters are typical figures of comedy. The king is a blustering and unreasonable figure, foolish in his repeated attempts to divest Bartholomew of his offending hats. His retinue includes buffoon types reminiscent of the cooks and clowns of Shakespeare:

the pompous prime minister, the ineffective and humorous wise men and magicians.

Bartholomew faces death bravely and calmly enough in his stolid way until he is saved, and in the nick of time, by the magic powers that brought him into danger in the first place. The final hats grow more and more magnificent until the vain and greedy king, behaving true to character, covets one for his own. He pays Bartholomew a substantial sum for the splendid five hundredth, places it over his crown, and is appeased at last. Arm-in-arm he and Bartholomew gaze out over the royal domain from the same vantage point, as equals. How such a reversal is accomplished is inherent in the comic structure itself. Everything moves toward the "happy ending" with the blocking characters converted to the hero's side.

The old tale of Cinderella is a prime example of the comic structure, its pattern enduring in displacements old and new and yet to come. It exemplifies comedy in the phase closest to romance for it involves magical manifestations and metamorphoses. Cinderella endures against the impossible odds of a cruel and unreasonable stepmother and her daughters who thwart her every wish and desire, including preventing her attendance at the prince's ball. Then her goodness is rewarded, the fairy godmother transforms her utterly. She must do as she is told (and she is used to that) and all will be well.

Cinderella at last is received into the society in which we all knew from the beginning she belonged; it is in effect a movement from illusion to reality. The illusion is always negative forces that must be dispelled, caused as they are by hypocrisy, disguise, and the like. Cinderella, of course, was really a princess in disguise, although it did not seem so at first. But the reader knows this, the prince recognizes it, and the king and queen receive her at the end as if she were a long-lost daughter. The character of Cinderella is the embodiment of a wish-fullment: virtue and goodness are rewarded; things turn out "as they should."

The comic form is a favorite of writers for children, found in countless traditional tales like "Beauty and the Beast" and "Snow White and the Seven Dwarfs," and in modern novels like Doris Gates's *Blue Willow* and Anne Holm's *North to Freedom*.

The main emphasis in comic literature, then, is on the creation of a new order. This is often achieved by equating the new and better world with the season of spring, a time of beginnings and renewal. The world at the end of a typical comedy is a new one, better and more ordered, freer and more merciful than the old order it replaced. The marriage and the happy ending typical of comedies is symbolic of the establishment of a new, more just society. The biblical Book of Revelation uses the marriage metaphor to symbolize an eventual happy ending to the story of mankind. A bride from earth, known variously as the New Jerusalem, the church, or the community of saints, is united with the redeemer and with him enters paradise. The central form of the comic story is symbolic of hope, of possibilities for new and renewed life, of the power of love.

To sum up: the main idea of romance, the first story, is adventure or action. An innocent, idealized person moves in a world beyond the ordinary and realistic world of experience and undergoes a quest involving a test of his human powers. The central idea of tragedy, the second story, is catastrophe or death befalling a hero who maintains those qualities humans consider heroic no matter what his fate. Tragedies may be romantic or ironic depending on whether they feature idealized characters or more realistic ones. The controlling idea of satire and irony is the absence of heroism and the presence of chaos, confusion, misery, and injustice—the world of experience. Satire attempts to change the unsatisfactory condition by revealing such things as hypocrisy through ridicule. The ironist simply shows things as he sees them and his point of view is a negative one. Comedy, the fourth story, moves out of ironic confusion with its central idea the human spirit's potential for renewal. It ends with a transformation of ironic chaos. The comic spirit is one of hope for the future and faith in human endurance over time.

The stories that man tells are parts of a single story. That one story is mankind's search for his human identity, a search that continues and will continue as long as there are people. It begins with an ideal world, moves through the less perfect world of human experience, and toward an ideal time when the perfection of the lost Eden is returned to us. This is the restoration promised in Revelation 21:4.

> And God shall wipe away all tears from their eyes; and there shall be no more death, neither sorrow, nor crying, neither shall there be any more pain: for the former things are passed away.

Literature, of course, is not religion. It does not address itself to belief. What it does provide is an imaginative vision. There are moments when we catch a glimpse of that perfect world. For it exists in the mind of the imaginative writer and in imaginations awakened by his words.

A knowledge of the structural principles of literature is reserved for the teacher. It should be obvious that this abstract framework is not something to be imposed upon the child as a piece of memory work. It is the teacher's business to know it and to structure the student's experiences with literature in such a way that the child will discover for himself the significant patterns in literature at the same time as he enjoys each literary experience for its own sake. The good teacher is one who can help students see significant patterns in facts. A teacher of literature has dual goals: that students will experience poems and stories with pleasure, and that they will grow in their knowledge of literature as a whole. The impact of literature upon the imagination is that much greater where there is an awareness of its unity.

Chapter 5

Theory into Practice

Our educational system may be compared to a pyramid. The elementary curriculum is the broad base on which the whole of the enormous structure rests and should provide adequate structural support for what is built upon it.

In recent years there has been a growing tendency to upgrade elementary education, to recognize that the younger student is capable of significant intellectual achievement. University scholars have increasingly participated in planning curricula for their disciplines that extend from kindergarten to graduate school, particularly in the areas of science and mathematics. From the famous Woods Hole Conference of 1959 came a key word that has dominated educational theory ever since. That key word is "structure."

Elementary education need not be intellectually insignificant, for once the structure of a discipline is understood *by the teacher*, it can be presented to the child in ways that are appropriate to his level of development. If the foundation of early learning is sound, later learning may be accomplished with greater ease and precision.

Basic Principles of Literary Criticism

Until now the study of literature has lacked a comprehensive theory that reveals its inherent structure. Many have believed that literature, because it is art and not science, cannot be considered structurally. Northrop Frye's theory provides proof that it can. Once the structural principles of literature are established, the teaching of literature, or criticism, can follow a deductive pattern, be consid-

45

erably simplified and clarified, and proceed progressively and systematically.

Frye's conceptual framework allows us to see the archetypal *shape* of literature as a whole, defining its boundaries much as a globe defines the earth for us. The framework produces a means of unifying and integrating discrete literary experiences, for within it each experience may be seen not only as an entity but as part of the total form of literature. There are fundamental principles to be derived from Frye's scheme that can inform the practice of elementary criticism. These basic principles may be summarized as follows:

The literary imagination seeks to suggest an identity between the human mind and the world outside it. The language of literature is associative, using figures of speech like the simile and metaphor to suggest this identity. In the logic of literature, therefore, two quite unlike things may be said to be like *each other or to* be *each other.*

Literature develops out of a center in mythology where the process of identification began with primitive man's efforts to identify himself imaginatively with animals, plants, and the forces of nature. His identity with these objects and energies appeared to him to be necessary for survival, or at least for a certain emotional security in a hostile world. With identity ("I am the eagle," "My mother is a sea nymph") came control—imaginative control over nature. The cycles of nature, everywhere apparent and consistent (sunrise, moonrise, the turning of seasons, births and deaths and more births), provided a pattern of repetition for stories of man's entire life—his quest for identity. The adventures, death, disappearance, and resurrection of the quester became the basis for our four generic literary plots: romance, tragedy, irony-satire, and comedy, and for the emotional moods of such forms as the lyric poem.

All stories are told within the structure *of one of the four generic plots no matter what* content *they may carry. Narratives may be examined as a series of displacements from mythology through romance to realism.*

Plots may be classified according to the quester's powers of action: in romance and tragedy these powers may be greater than those of the ordinary human being; in comedy they are much the same; in irony they are less.

All of literature is underlaid by two structures or thought constructs: the cyclical and the dialectical. The presence of the natural cycle provides a rising movement associated with spring and a falling movement associated with fall and winter. These movements are the structural principles of comedy (rising) and tragedy (falling). There is also a dialectic in myth, the first literature, which projects a paradise above our world and a hell below it. These constructs appear in literature as the idealized world of romance and the frustrated, suffering world of irony and satire.

The cyclical and dialectical structures underlie all literary imagery forming a framework within which all literary works, individually and together, represent man's imaginative efforts to recapture an original lost sense of identity with his surroundings. The quester's story connects with the two opposite limits of man's imagination: the quester is someone who, in our dreams, we would like to be identified with; his enemies and negative experiences are the stuff of our nightmares and represent what we would like to avoid. The hero's quest is an effort to regain identity, to restore the harmony and perfection of the lost paradise or golden age of man's imagination. "Identity" of course refers not only to discovering his name or paternity (though this is often the case on the surface of many stories), but also to reestablishing a lost unity or oneness with nature or some social group.

In literary imagery certain seasons of the year and times of day are characteristically related to happiness, youth, and beginnings; while others are related to sorrow, age, and endings. Certain colors and natural settings are used recurrently to reflect particular moods and atmospheres. The two dreams of man are expressed symbolically in his literature: at one limit of his desire is the wasteland or wilderness; at the other is his vision of a garden or paradise. Certain animals, birds, and natural phenomena are associated positively with man's hopes, dreams, and desires, and others negatively, with what he rejects as undesirable.

A consideration of literary works in terms of the cyclical and dialectical structures that underlie them provides a sense of the interrelatedness of all literature. Since all of the themes, characters, and stories of literature are related to achieve literature's common purpose of identifying the human mind with the world outside it, there are to be found analogies and resemblances among all works of literature.

These basic understandings concerning the structure of literature provide a deductive framework for the teacher. The student is led toward these understandings inductively. With the deductive framework to guide him, the teacher structures *learning sequences* that give the children scope for asking questions, forming their own conclusions, and testing these against evidence.

Structuring Learning Sequences in Literary Criticism

The learning sequence includes selecting literature that will suit the experience, intellectual development, and preferences of children, while illustrating the concept of understanding to be developed in the course of a particular sequence.

The works selected for presentation in class are presented as works of art, interpreted most often orally, with the accent on experience rather than analysis. Discussions follow, in a classroom climate of respect for the individual and his responses. By means of question and comment, the teacher guides the course of the discussion in such a way that children reach, by a process of discovery, some understanding of the literary principle the sequence is designed to illustrate. The success of a learning sequence will depend in large measure upon the teacher's ability to guide group discussion in such a way that the concept or understanding around which the sequence centers will be discoverable by and comprehensible to the students.

Discussion as an Aid to Learning

A learning sequence properly structured provides children with the opportunity to learn for themselves, to discover, to test their ideas against those of others, to become absorbed in study through active participation, to engage in both convergent and divergent thinking. The value of dialogue between children and their peers cannot be overstressed. James Moffett describes adequate discussion as a *learned* process of

> amending, appending, diverging, converging, elaborating, summarizing, and many other things. Most of all, it is an external social process that each member gradually internalizes as a personal thought process: he begins to think in the ways his group talks. Not only does he take unto himself the vocabulary, usage, and syntax of others and synthesize new creations out of their various styles, points of view, and attitudes; he also structures his thinking into mental operations resembling the operations of the group interactions. If the group amends, challenges, elaborates, and qualifies together, each member begins to do so alone in his inner speech.*

Discussion that is structured and purposeful and at the same time free and relaxed facilitates the learning of specific literary concepts while it provides an opportunity for perfecting communication skills and being heard as an individual.

*James Moffett, *A Student-Centered Language Arts Curriculum, Grades K-6: A Handbook for Teachers* (Boston: Houghton Mifflin, 1968), p. 46.

Guidelines for Successful Discussion

A distinction should be made between small- and large-group discussion. Whole-class discussion, unless it follows discussion by small groups, is unlikely to be more than an extemporaneous exchange among a few. Only a limited number of students in a class of average size can participate at once, comments are likely to be addressed to the teacher and not to other pupils, and unengaged minds are apt to wander. Children should be taught to discuss together in groups of no more than six or eight.

The process of discussion is something that must be *taught*; children cannot be expected to proceed with it profitably without specific guidance. Discussion has two major emphases: courtesy and participation. The child is introduced to the ritual exchange of give-and-take that genuine discussion requires. He learns to listen, to wait his turn, to assimilate and weigh what he has heard, and to build upon this when he speaks. The teacher works from the first encounter with a new class to establish a climate of mutual respect where ideas and opinions are courteously listened to, where one is helped toward understanding rather than criticized for the lack of it. The process is a developmental one with first experiences carefully planned for success.

With the teacher's guidance, the children themselves can evolve the ground rules that will govern their discussions. The first small-group activity for a class might well be a session in which groups work together to evolve these rules, pooling their ideas in a large-group sharing session at the end, and preparing a final list cooperatively for the guidance of all.

Discussion groups for literary criticism are likely to be best if they are heterogeneous and their composition frequently changed. Slow learners should have the opportunity to work with faster learners in an atmosphere of mutual help and support; the least articulate and the most verbally facile will mutually benefit from working together. Common interests, personal preferences, and individual needs will also determine the composition of groups. If there is a child as group leader, the role should be rotated.

At first the teacher may lead the discussion, working with a group while the rest of the class is engaged in other activities. Later he may circulate from group to group, working first with one and then another. As soon as possible he should abandon the role of leader and assume that of guide or resource person. Children should be encouraged to address their remarks to each other and not to the teacher when he joins their group.

As a guide and resource person the teacher has two functions: he helps to facilitate the group process itself and at the same time answers questions and supplies subject matter information the children may require. He should avoid offering quantities of unsolicited information, but he may, with judicious questioning, bring forth a request for information that he sees is needed. In facilitating the discussion process he gives the children needed experience in listening to hear each other out. Long-winded soliloquizers are good-naturedly curtailed; interruptions are discouraged with a tactful comment or hand gesture. As he visits each group, the teacher, with comments and questions: (a) encourages participation: "Mary, we haven't heard from you on this"; (b) handles the monopolizer with a tactful but firm comment such as "Wait a moment, John; Ruth hasn't finished yet"; (c) pacifies the one who has introduced an irrelevancy by suggesting that his idea should be noted for discussion at another time; (d) helps groups to draw conclusions and summarize their ideas; and (e) helps with definitional problems or more serious problems of personal relations. Throughout he provides a model for the students with his tact, courtesy, and genuine willingness to listen to another's ideas.

The more structured discussion may grow spontaneously from the comments and questions of the children. For example, after a fifth-grade class has heard a story, they might raise questions about the ending. A number feel strongly that "it couldn't have happened that way," that the author "fooled them," that "it doesn't make sense." The teacher might structure the ensuing discussion with: "Let's talk this problem over in smaller groups so everyone will get a chance to say what he thinks." (The teacher goes to the board.) "Now, what are some of the questions you have been asking? Let's jot down the main ones and you can try to answer them yourselves in your groups."

No discussion should be allowed to drag on interminably until the bored participants, talked out, turn to paper planes, spitballs, and harassment of others for solace. Three to five minutes will be sufficient for most questions, particularly in the beginning; but the experience, level of maturity, and interest of the class, as well as the purpose of the discussion, will be the teacher's guides in establishing time limits.

At the end of the small-group discussion, groups may be assembled together to pool ideas and *to evaluate their experience with the discussion process itself.* A leader or spokesman may report for the group; if groups have made use of recorders, the recorder might make the report, in more advanced classes making use of notes.

Each discussion should have a specific purpose to guide it or a specific problem to be discussed in the course of it. As he structures learning sequences in literary criticism by means of discussion, the teacher has the deductive scheme in mind to which the inductive presentation is related; the children reach an understanding of literary principles through a process of discovery that is facilitated by the interchange that the teacher guides and structures.

Principles into Procedure

In order to teach literature, the teacher must be a student of it. The understanding of the basic principles of literary theory is of little value without a broad knowledge of children's literature. To structure learning sequences the teacher needs to know what poems and stories will be best suited to each level. College courses in children's literature together with wide reading, ranging from picture books through novels written for early adolescents, will supply this knowledge. Reference books such as May Hill Arbuthnot's *Children and Books* are helpful but the information they supply is never a substitute for reading the literature itself. A collection of the calibre of *Anthology of Children's Literature* by Edna Johnson and others is useful in providing a perspective on the broad field of children's literature. Texts and anthologies like those mentioned provide comprehensive bibliographies of inestimable help to teachers in selecting their reading.

To teach criticism it is not necessary to set up rigid courses of study to be "covered" in a given year. The literature used as examples in literary discussions and as the basis for creative response is all of the literature the children encounter, in school and out. It includes the books read independently by individuals and those shared through classroom reading. It includes the stories and poems selected by the teacher and shared with the whole group or smaller groups within it through reading aloud.

From the earliest age and through all the elementary grades children should be read to regularly, taking in literature by the ear as well as the eye. Children will never discover the wide and varied wonders to be found in literature by gazing at the spines of books in the library. They need the guidance of an interested, sympathetic adult who, by enthusiastically sharing all kinds of stories and poems, takes them well inside the vast world of literature. Left to themselves they are likely to explore only its outer boundaries or isolated areas here and there within it.

When literature is considered in terms of its structural principles, the approach to its study is broader and freer than study that centers in the content of individual works. It does not emphasize the close analysis of specific items in a prescribed text. It takes into account all of a student's reading and listening. The true business of criticism is not the pursuit of answers to a list of questions that test basic comprehension. Comprehension of literature occurs on many levels and some of it may not be translated into discursive language. Stories and poems must of course be understood in the sense of being intelligible. But it is unlikely that children will choose to read much that is incomprehensible to them. And it is unlikely that sensitive teachers will read to them for very long something that is above or beyond them. Criticism expands knowledge of literature in a natural way, giving the student the opportunity to think of literature in terms of all of his reading rather than merely in terms of items in a reader.

Criticism does not only involve the student's experience with literature. It means dealing with his total verbal experience as well. Much of this experience is sub-literary, found in television serials and advertisements, comics and magazines, films and pop songs. The points of contact between literary and sub-literary experiences need to be kept in mind, the whole considered in literary terms. Archetypal characters, images, and plots found in literature are found as well in sub-literary forms. Students who are helped to see these resemblances will be pleased to see that literature is not something that is associated only with classrooms. Furthermore, they will, by relating the two together, see how the mythology of television drama and advertisements copies that of literature. Through comparison they will gradually see how the one is a shoddy form, a rival mythology determined to capture their imaginations for its own purposes. Powers of discernment will not be developed all at once, but they will never be developed at all if children do not have an early awareness of how the mass media functions to condition them.

Literary criticism, then, involves a consideration of all the literature a student encounters and all of his other verbal experience as well. In the next two chapters poetry and story are considered separately to facilitate the detailing of procedure in literary criticism. In actual practice they cannot be separated from each other, nor can they be separated from nonliterary experience. In genuine criticism the unity of literature is preserved and the scope of its influence made clear.

Chapter 6

The Study of Poetry

Young children are natural poets. They *move* to language, skipping or stomping or strutting to the rhythm of sounds. A six-year-old hears a snatch of adult conversation and appropriates a word or two, whirling his arms as he chants: "Involuted! Convoluted! Involuted! Convoluted!"

They savor words, tasting them, rolling them on their tongues in the rhymes and jingles that are part of their games and communication with each other:

> Julius Caesar
> The Roman geezer,
> Squashed his wife with a
> lemon squeezer.*

To children rhyme is both funny and remarkable in itself. A nine-year-old says of the following bit of nonsense, "I think what's so clever about this is the way it all rhymes."

> Mrs. White had a fright
> In the middle of the night
> She saw a ghost eating toast
> Half-way up the lamp post.†

They are delighted by a word with two uses: "What runs but never walks?" (*Answer:* A stream.) Puns of any kind please their fancies, as do word plays and conundrums: "What is the difference between a big black cloud and a lion with a toothache?" (*Answer:* One pours with rain and the other roars with pain.)

---

*Iona and Peter Opie, *The Lore and Language of School Children* (New York: Oxford University Press, 1959), p. 20.
†*Ibid.*, p. 17.

Riddles are children's special delight. And riddles are like the metaphors of poetic thought: something is imaginatively described in terms of something else as the teeth and gums are in the following:

Thirty white horses
Upon a red hill
Now they stamp,
Now they chomp,
Now they stand still.

In poetry language is tapped for rhythm, rhyme, double meanings, unusual juxtapositions of sound; it is used to create images. The best of poetry appeals directly to one or more of the senses. It is a concrete mode of expression as well as a remarkable and delightful one. Since their lore and daily language (chants, taunt-songs, word plays, and the like) show that children and poets have much in common, it is foolish—and dangerous—for teachers to deny children poetry. In school poetry is commonly regarded as a frill, an utter nonessential and children are often deprived of it. This deprivation is evident in many children's dull, unrhythmic, grace-less writing. The lilt, the surge and thunder of verse, the expert timing of the rise and fall of cadences, when they are absorbed over the course of time, do more to develop writing ability than books full of exercises.

In one experiment, children whose language classes for many weeks were devoted entirely to an *oral* reading of the *Iliad* in Richmond Lattimore's translation wrote "epic" poems of their own. One eleven-year-old, inspired by the historical novels of Rosemary Sutcliff that he had been reading, created an original plot centered around Marius, a young galley slave. An excerpt from his poem is proof that he had absorbed the rhythms and imagery of the *Iliad.*

As he entered the hold, they sprang upon him,
As lions spring upon the unwary buck,
And they grappled with him and bound him.
When morning dawned the boy awoke
To feel sharp pain in his head
Where they had struck him with a wooden club;
Where bonds had been, there was now a shackle,
And he was chained to a bench with others, unlucky,
A slave in the galleys of
King Solomon's Navy.

As the days became weeks,
And the weeks months,
He learned the ways of the rowers
From the man Jason, who was his friend.
So also he learned to eat the black bread;
And, as the jackals fight for the scraps
On the bony carcass that is left to them
By the lions, so he fought
For the scraps left to them by his master.
But, above all, he learned to hate.
. . .

Laurence Woodruff

It may be difficult for those who are surrounded by masses of print that passes for prose to believe that any other mode of expression has validity. It will be even more difficult for them to believe that reading poetry is the best way to learn to write prose. Still, all teaching involves a certain measure of faith and there will be those willing to be persuaded.

They will be the ones who put poetry first, not last, in the language arts curriculum. In the interests of a balanced diet it will not be all the literary nourishment their students receive. But it will be served in large portions and never only as dessert.

Choosing Poetry for Children

There is one rule of thumb for the choice of poetry to be used with children: it should be the best available. It is essential that it be "poetic" in the sense of being imagistic and rhythmic. The work of chatty poets who write versified prose should be avoided as well as the nonpoetic verse that is written especially, and badly, for children in the form of sentimental ditties. Poems should employ metaphor and image effectively and delightfully; they should have strong sensory appeal; many should illustrate patterns of repetition and rhyme; all poems chosen for use with children should speak to the child at his level of understanding and experience, but they should also broaden experience and stretch the imagination with new concepts and fresh ways of looking at things.

Riddles are examples of pure imagery and they should have a central place at every grade level in the elementary school. In riddles and conundrums, rhymed or unrhymed, the poet's way of looking at the world is clearly evident; he uses analogy and association with telling effect. Early experience with epigrammatic say-ings, concise and compact like the proverb, helps the child to under-stand the economy inherent in poetic expression. Many proverbs and epigrams are highly imagistic or metaphorical, illustrating at once two primary qualities of poetry.

Although it is the teacher's responsibility to bring the best of poetry to children, he should remember that he is choosing *for* chil-dren and, therefore, try to read and listen to poems as a child would read and listen. What delights a child may seem simplistic to the adult, but delight is an important ingredient in poetry programs for children. The wise teacher is one who learns from the pupils, encouraging them to share their own favorites whether they are from an anthology or from the oral lore of childhood: jingles, chants, game-songs, taunt-songs, word games, even the lively singing com-mercials learned from television and radio. Choosing poetry to use with children can never become an academic exercise.

Poems may be rhymed or unrhymed; they may be stories or lyrics; they may be old or new; they may be on any subject that might interest the children. Foolproof introductions to poetry are those that will lead the child to regard vigorous rhythm and meta-phorical thought as a simple and direct form of utterance. Such introductions would include ballads; works suitable for children by such major poets as Emily Dickinson, William Blake, Christina Rossetti, and Gerard Manley Hopkins; and the work of modern writ-ers of verse for children: Eleanor Farjeon, Walter de la Mare, David McCord, Harry Behn, Leland Jacobs, James Reeves, Dorothy Aldis, Laura E. Richards, and Eve Merriam, to name a few.

Poems may be classified in numerous ways. In anthologies they are grouped according to theme and content: nature poems, animal poems, poems about fairies, poems about love, poems about city life. When thinking in terms of archetypal criticism, however, the teacher will go beyond these arbitrary classifications to even broader ones. To foster the understanding of poems as part of the whole of literature, essentially the expression of man's search for identity between the objective and inner worlds of his experience, the teacher will consider poems as they fit into such classifications as these:

  —Poems that express wishes, dreams, and desires, usually
   of an existence or circumstance better than one presently
   being experienced.
  —Poems that deal with the life and death of humans, animals, birds, and nature.

—Poems that pinpoint a moment in time, a place, a wish, or desire.

—Poems that are simply expressions of feeling or emotion.

—Poems that are rhythmic and verbal representations of work or play.

Presenting Poetry to Children

Poetry as a Part of Daily Experience

When the little child is accepted as a rhythmic being, poetry will be seen and encouraged as a valid means of expression and not regarded as a mere frill or recreational activity for the time, free of the "real work" of the classroom. Poetry cannot be relegated to an occasional lesson in its appreciation. As Leland Jacobs, eminent educator and writer of children's verse, says, it must become an integral part of daily living, embedded in the ritual of the classroom. The effective teacher will have poems on the tip of his tongue for all occasions: if someone has new shoes, a new baby brother, or a case of the sniffles; if the first robin appears, or the first flake of snow, he will be ready at a moment's notice to bring forth an appropriate poem or know where to find one to read aloud.

The Importance of Oral Presentation

The infant who gets bounced on somebody's knee to the rhythm of "Ride a cock horse" does not need a footnote telling him that Banbury Cross is twenty miles northeast of Oxford. He does not need the information that "cross" and "horse" make (at least in the pronunciation he is most likely to hear) not a rhyme but an assonance. He does not need the value-judgment that the repetition of "horse" in the first two lines indicates a rather tin ear on the part of the composer. All he needs is to get bounced. If he is, he is beginning to develop a response to poetry in the place where it ought to start.*

In the elementary school years, and even before formal education begins, children should experience poetry orally. Children develop an antipathy toward poetry only after they become independent readers when there is a greater possibility that poetry will

*Northrop Frye, *The Well-Tempered Critic* (Bloomington: Indiana University Press, 1963), p. 25.

become for them nothing more than static rows of print on a page, perhaps the subject of analysis and dissection, or something that they must memorize under pressure. The silent treatment of poetry can never result, at least for the young child, in an appreciation and enjoyment of poetry. Poetry should be read aloud, as effectively as possible, by the teacher who, in most cases, will be the best oral interpreter the child will encounter. Recordings may be used for variety, but they are never a substitute for the live performance that involves direct sharing between a teacher and a class. Children should be encouraged but not coerced to read aloud to others, with preparation always preceding performance. All oral interpreters should prepare their presentations, selecting only those poems that they most enjoy, for these will be the best read.

As often as possible, the oral experience with poetry should be accompanied with a physical response. Children should repeat lines and verses that have natural appeal, perhaps joining in on the refrain as they listen to a verse such as:

> A farmer went trotting upon his grey mare,
>   Bumpety, bumpety, bump!
> With his daughter behind him so rosy and fair,
>   Lumpety, Lumpety, lump!
>
> A raven cried, Croak! and they all tumbled down,
>   Bumpety, bumpety, bump!
> The mare broke her knees and the farmer his crown,
>   Lumpety, lumpety, lump!
>
> The mischievous raven flew laughing away,
>   Bumpety, bumpety, bump!
> And vowed he would serve them the same the next day,
>   Lumpety, lumpety, lump!

Moving to the rhythms of the poem is to be encouraged. It is natural for little children to gallop to "Ride a cock horse," walk with "To market, to market," march smartly to "The Grand Old Duke of York," or hop in time with A. A. Milne's "Hoppity." For older children it is fun to act out the action words of a poem: slink, dance, creep, rush, and the like.

Poems may be acted out as well as moved to, their rhythmic qualities brought to life through physical response. The acting may be representational, with children taking turns miming each episode of, say, A. A. Milne's "The King's Breakfast," or it may be free movement, to a lyric such as Ella Young's "Rain."

Dancing dancing down the street
Comes the rain on silver feet:
O hush, O hush,
For the wind is fluting a song.

Little flute of the wind,
Little flute of the wind,
Little flute of the wind
Play on.

Silver feet of the rain
Come again, come again,
Come with a fluting song.

Avoiding Verse Vivisection

Poems should be respected and enjoyed for what they are—imaginative constructs that are not translatable into utilitarian prose. No effort should be made to extract what is often erroneously called a poem's "real" meaning.

The question, "What does it mean?" has no place in the study of poetry at any level, because it fails to make a necessary distinction between imaginative and discursive writing. What the poet meant to say is, literally, the poem itself; what he meant to say in any given passage is, in its literal meaning, part of the poem. It is a fruitless and wasteful procedure to translate or try to translate a poem into discursive commentary. Such teaching distorts the child's experience, giving him the confusing and erroneous belief that poetry exists only as a distortion of prose. Instead, the child should be helped to know, by means of the best examples and with enjoyment and experimentation, that poetry is a valid mode of thought. The poem is experienced as a whole, its "meaning" accepted as part of the whole.

Leland Jacobs, in his famous example of how a poem may be destroyed by treating it as discourse, quotes to classes of teachers "The Goblin" and mimics the absurdity of the misguided teacher who would ask his pupils such questions as "What does it mean?" "Where, children, does the goblin live?" "How many things does he do?" "Can you name each one in its proper order?"

THE GOBLIN

A goblin lives in *our* house, in *our* house, in *our* house,
A goblin lives in *our* house all the year round.
He bumps

And he jumps
And he thumps
And he stumps.
He knocks
And he rocks
And he rattles at the locks.
A goblin lives in *our* house, in *our* house, in *our* house,
A goblin lives in *our* house all the year round.

Rose Fyleman

If a poem requires considerable explication and commentary before, during, or after the reading of it, it is probably the wrong choice for a particular group. Poems should stand by themselves, requiring few if any props, at eye level with the child, representative or suggestive of something within his experience. Occasionally it may be necessary to clarify a concept or offer the meaning of a word before reading a poem to a class but, in general, even this practice should be avoided. A better plan is to encourage the children's own questions about points that may bewilder them.

The emphasis is upon delight rather than dissection. In Archibald MacLeish's words, "a poem should not mean but be." "It takes children a long time," say the Opies, "before they cease to be amazed that one word can have more than one meaning." Certainly a literary education worthy of the name should see to it that this amazement with the delightful things that words can do is fostered and made to last a lifetime. This can never be accomplished through unpalatable practices such as vivesection. Children's initial experiences with poetry must center in delight. Only if this is so are more analytical procedures possible and palatable as the child grows older. And even these must be planned to enhance and not destroy the essence of the poetic experience.

Archetypal Literary Criticism Applied to Poetry

> Archetypes are the things which recur in literature and archetypal criticism . . . is an attempt to see what the literary context of a work of literature is . . . to see what meaning can be thrown on the individual work from its context in literature.*

*Author's interview with Northrop Frye, August 27, 1970.

A teacher of literature wants his pupils to experience poetry with pleasure; he also wants their knowledge of literature to develop systematically. Although discursive explication and commentary about poems is to be avoided in the elementary school, this does not mean that the young child's experiences with poetry cannot be fitted meaningfully into a critical framework that will allow his sense of literature as an order of words to grow and develop with focus and direction. Through his *choice and arrangement* of certain selections of poetry, the teacher can, through *guidance of the children's questions and discussion,* help even the youngest child to begin to see for himself how each poem is one of the larger family of all literary works.

Significant learning takes place when the student goes beyond a consideration of detail and specific content to become aware of an overall pattern or structure to which he may relate discrete experiences. The student proceeds inductively, within a deductive framework established by the teacher, to see relationships for himself. In the case of poetry, for instance, the teacher will help him to see in what ways poetic expression is a unique mode of thought with its own techniques and characteristics.

Discursive writing describes the world, but imaginative literature uses language in a way that connects our minds with the objective world in an effort to associate and identify the mind with what goes on in the world beyond it. The simile and the metaphor are the units of identification. They make of the objective world something that is essentially human in shape and try to recapture, in words, man's original lost sense of identity with his surroundings. The limit of the imagination is a totally human world where all things are identical with man's mind or absorbed within it.

The logic of metaphor which insists that "this *is* that" is not the logic of reason; it is, rather, an *imaginative* logic that illustrates how the poet goes beyond nature to show a world absorbed and possessed by the human mind. In poetry it is not only legitimate but highly desirable to tell the "truth" by means of analogy and association—truth that need not be defended or refuted in discursive terms because it cannot be. Poetry that makes use of associative language effectively with suggestive images that make their own sense should be regarded by the child as a valid mode of expression. If he is able to grasp this basic understanding of poetry in the elementary school, his problems of understanding or accepting the "difficult" images of the poets he will study in high school and beyond will be minimized.

Children should become aware of the logic of metaphorical language in literature, not by collecting similes and metaphors as if they were so many colorful pebbles, but by seeing for themselves, as they read and write, the worth and value of using concrete and sensory imagery to express ideas. Children employ metaphor in their natural expression and are skilled users of slang, which might be called the poetry of everyday speech. When their natural propensities are fostered and channeled and they are encouraged to make use of analogy and identity for precise expression, their own writing will benefit and they will take additional delight in the use of such expression by others.

A Learning Sequence for the
Upper Elementary Grades

Aim of the sequence: In this example the teacher's principal aim is to lead the children to an understanding that certain patterns of imagery are associated with the expression of happy and sad feelings. The children have experienced a number of poems of their own and the teacher's choosing. Included in the teacher's selections might be poems like the following, representative of both moods and illustrative of the point he wants the children to grasp.

Poems included in the sequence.

LAUGHING SONG

When the green woods laugh with the voice of joy,
And the dimpling stream runs laughing by;
When the air does laugh with our merry wit,
And the green hill laughs with the noise of it;

When the meadows laugh with lively green,
And the grasshopper laughs in the merry scene,
When Mary and Susan and Emily
With their sweet round mouths sing "Ha, Ha, He!"

When the painted birds laugh in the shade,
Where our table with cherries and nuts is spread,
Come live and be merry and join with me,
To sing the sweet chorus of "Ha, Ha, He!"

William Blake

HERE WE COME A-PIPING

Here we come a-piping,
In Springtime and in May;
Green fruit a-ripening,
And Winter fled away.
The Queen she sits upon the strand,
Fair as a lily, white as a wand;
Seven billows on the sea,
Horses riding fast and free,
And bells beyond the sand.

Traditional

CITY AUTUMN

The air breathes frost. A thin wind beats
Old dust and papers down gray streets
And blows brown leaves with curled-up edges
At frightened sparrows on window ledges.
A snow-flake falls like an errant feather:
A vagabond draws his cloak together,
And an old man totters past with a cane
Wondering if he'll see Spring again.

Joseph Moncure March

DARK GIRL

Easy on your drums,
Easy wind and rain,
And softer on your horns,
She will not dance again.

Come easy little leaves
Without a ghost of sound
From the China trees
To the fallow ground.

Easy, easy drums
And sweet leaves overhead,
Easy wind and rain;
Your dancing girl is dead.

Arna Bontemps

In Time of Silver Rain

In time of silver rain
The earth
Puts forth new life again,
Green grasses grow
And flowers lift their heads,
And over all the plain
The wonder spreads   ,
    Of life,
    Of life,
    Of Life!

In time of silver rain
The butterflies
Lift silken wings
To catch a rainbow cry,
And trees put forth
New leaves to sing
In joy beneath the sky
As down the roadway
Passing boys and girls
Go singing, too,
In time of silver rain
    When spring
    And life
    Are new.

Langston Hughes

Discussion: The learning sequence proceeds as follows: the children have experienced a number of poems, and now, as preparation for writing their own, they are discussing them, the initial discussion involving the entire class. This is, of course, an "ideal" dialogue: these answers will not come so easily from most children. It shows the importance of the teacher's questions in eliciting responses.

Teacher: Think of the poems we have shared lately. What were some of the subjects they dealt with?
Pupils: —They talked about people.
       —And animals.
       —A lot of them were nature poems.
       —I think most of them expressed feelings.

—They all do! Every poem expresses some kind of feeling. That's what it's all about.

Teacher: What feelings do they express?
Pupils: —Sadness, sometimes, like in the poem "Dark Girl." It's gloomy, because, after all, she's dead.
            —So is "City Autumn" sad. It makes you think of dreary days. There's not much hope in it.
            —Most of the poems we heard were happy, though.
            —Yeah. Like "Laughing Song" and that other one by Hughes, I think it was . . .
            —I know. It's called "In Time of Silver Rain."
            —Most of the poems we read by E. E. Cummings were happy, like the one that starts, "In just-spring."
            —I guess you could say that most poems either make you feel sad or happy; some are stronger than others.

Teacher: Think of some of the happy poems you know. What season of the year are they usually describing?
Pupils: —Spring!
            —Or summer!
            —They're nearly always talking about the coming of spring or summer.
            —The sadder poems are usually talking about fall, when the leaves are falling and things are dying. Like "City Autumn."
            —Or it's winter and cold and everything is dead.

Teacher: Do you think you could arrange the poems you know according to the seasons?
Pupils: —All of them? Some of them don't mention a season.
            —They may not mention one directly, but the idea is there.
            —I think that's stretching it a little!

Teacher: Well, let's see if it is. *(The teacher sketches a circle on the board and divides it into four parts, labeling each respectively spring, summer, autumn, winter.*)* Why don't you get into groups of six: just pull your chairs

*This is illustrated in the drawing on page 21. It is important for students to realize that the purpose of this circle and the classifying of poems is *not simply to categorize them,* but *to reveal* to images that *recur* throughout them all, differentiating them yet *uniting* them in one imaginative vision.

around in a circle with the people nearest you, and see whether you can classify the poems you know according to the four seasons, *whether they mention the seasons directly or not.* We'll pool your findings later.

Follow-up: The next learning sequence, evolving naturally out of this one, might be a consideration of the kinds of images from nature that are associated with happy poems and sad poems. Trees, gardens, fields, and flowers are associated with happy visions in most cases. Falling leaves, rocky landscapes, and harsh cold winds are usually associated with melancholy poems. The children might be asked what kind of images and what natural settings they would choose if they were going to write about death, say, or injustice, or pleasure and happy times.

A Learning Sequence for the Lower Elementary Grades

Aim of the sequence: Here the teacher leads young children toward an awareness that the literary imagination always seeks to suggest an identity between the human mind and the world outside it, and that it does so by means of metaphor, the language of identification: "This is that."

Discussion: Here again is an "ideal" dialogue with sample responses the teacher could try to elicit from students.

Teacher: Just before class I saw Peter galloping along the schoolyard.

Pupils: —I was a horse, a really fast race horse like the one I saw Saturday.
—It feels good to gallop.

Teacher: I'd like you all to act out for me what it's like to feel good. Let's push back the seats so we have room to move. Now, *show* me with your whole body what it's like to feel really good, really happy. *(Pupils proceed with movement mimes, some moving in place, others moving around the room.)* I saw lots of happy people just now. Mary, you seemed to be flying . . .

Pupils: —I was. I was a bird!
              —I was a cloud!
              —I was a rabbit and Tom was too; we were chasing each
              other.
              —I was sunshine. Did you see me?
              —I was a tree getting blown by the wind.
              —I was flying a kite in the wind.

Teacher: Everybody acted out feeling happy by being something
              else. I wonder why?

Pupils: —That's just the way you do it.
              —If I just stand here feeling happy, you couldn't really
              tell. I had to pretend I was a leaf flying around. That's
              what it feels like to be feeling good.

Teacher: Listen to this:

SWING SONG

Oh, I've discovered
A happy thing!
For every game
There's a song to sing,
Sometimes with words
Sometimes without,
It's easy to tell
What a song's about
From only a humming
Like wind at noon,
It needn't be even
Half a tune
If only it goes
With what you do,
If what you do
Is exactly true,
Or anyway if
It seems to you.
The time I discovered
This wonderful thing
I really was swinging
In a swing.
And the song I was singing
Was just as true

For all the flying
Sky-things too,
For seagulls and eagulls
And bees and bugs
And arrows and sparrows,
Enchanted rugs,
Clouds and balloons,
Balloons and bees—
A backward humming
A forward breeze,
Swinging without
Any tune you please.

Harry Behn

Pupils: —Feeling happy is like swinging on a swing.
—It's like a song going on inside you.
—Like the poem we know about the kite.

Teacher: Will you all say that one for me? I'll start and you join in. *(They say together the following little poem that they have learned.)*

A KITE

I often sit and wish that I
Could be a kite up in the sky,
And ride upon the breeze and go
Whichever way I chanced to blow.

Teacher: In order to show what it's like to feel happy, you have to use a comparison. Feeling happy is like other things. Is that what you're telling me? *(Teacher records responses on the board, on a chart, or on tape.)*
Pupils: —Yes! Feeling happy is humming a song.
—Feeling happy is a bird.
—Happy is sunshine.
—Happy is wind.
—Happy is butterflies in your stomach.
—Happy is like a big red balloon.

Teacher: Do you know what? You've made a poem just by saying what happy is like. You did just what the poets do. Do you know what I mean by that?

Pupils: —We said that things were like other things.
            —We said things *were* other things.
            —We said a feeling like happy was like something you
              can smell.
            —Or hear.
            —Or even taste.
Teacher: Let's read our poem.

Follow-up: Subsequent learning sequences would further develop the idea of metaphor to identify things other than emotions. The book *Hailstones and Halibut Bones* and the film made from the book would be suitable literary material for this purpose, used to teach the concept of metaphor and to stimulate similar compositions by the children.* The following is an excerpt from *Hailstones and Halibut Bones:*

WHAT IS WHITE?

White is a dove
And lily of the valley
And a puddle of milk
Spilled in an alley—
A ship's sail
A kite's tail
A wedding veil
Hailstones and
Halibut bones
And some people's telephones.

Mary LeDuc O'Neill

Structuring Additional
Learning Sequences with Poetry

Imagery I: Selected poems will help the children to see that many poems are involved with wishes, dreams, and desires. The teacher's stimulus for such a sequence would include questions such as the following: *What kinds of things do people wish for? When we think of things becoming better than they are, what direction do we associate with "getting better," down or up? What seasons of the year or times of day are usually associated with getting one's*

*The film is available, for purchase only, from Sterling Educational Films, 241 E. 34th St., New York, N.Y. 10016.

wish or realizing a dream? Poems such as the following might be included in the learning sequence:

HAIKU

When my canary
flew away, that was the end
of spring in my house.

WILD GEESE

I heard the wild geese flying
In the dead of night,
With beat of wings and crying
I heard the wild geese flying,
And dreams in my heart sighing
Followed their northward flight.
I hear the wild geese flying
In the dead of night.

Elinor Chipp

UP IN THE AIR

Zooming across the sky
Like a great bird you fly,
Airplane,
Silvery white
In the light

Turning and twisting in air,
When shall I ever be there,
Airplane,
Piloting you
Far in the blue?

James E. Tippett

FIREFLY

A little light is going by,
Is going up to see the sky,
A little light with wings.

I never could have thought of it.
To have a little bug all lit
And made to go on wings.

Elizabeth Madox Roberts

STARS

O, sweep of stars over Harlem Streets
O, little breath of oblivion that is night.
      A city building
      To a mother's song.
      A city dreaming
      To a lullaby.
Reach up your hand, dark boy, and take a star.
Out of the little breath of oblivion
      That is night
      Take just
      One star.

Langston Hughes

ROADS GO EVER EVER ON

Roads go ever ever on,
Over rock and under tree,
By caves where never sun has shone,
By streams that never find the sea;
Over snow by winter sown,
And through the merry flowers of June,
Over grass and over stone,
And under mountains in the moon.

J. R. R. Tolkien

DECEMBER

A little boy stood on the corner
And shoveled bits of dirty, soggy snow
Into the sewer—
With a jagged piece of tin.
He was helping spring come.

Sanderson Vanderbilt

Imagery II: Man's "dreams" and "nightmares" may be examined through his poetry. The teacher's questions to stimulate this learning sequence might include: *What images of nature are associated with happy dreams? with nightmares? What seasons and times of day are associated with dreams? with nightmares? Of the city and the country, which place is likely to be associated with dreams? with nightmares?* Poems such as the following would be included in the learning sequence:

A CITY PARK

Timidly
Against a background of brick tenements
Some trees spread their branches skyward.
They are thin and sapless,
They are bent and weary—
Tamed with captivity;
And they huddle behind the fence
Swaying helplessly before the wind,
Forward and backward
Like a group of panicky deer
Caught in a cage.

Alter Brody

TRANSCONTINENT

Where the cities end, the
dumps grow the oil-can shacks
from Portland, Maine,

to Seattle, Broken
cars rust in Troy, New York,
and Cleveland Heights,

On the train, the people
eat candy bars, and watch,
or fall asleep.

When they look outside and
see the cars and shacks, they know
they're nearly there.

Donald Hall

HEAVEN–HAVEN

I have desired to go
    Where springs not fail,
To fields where flies no sharp and sided hail
    And a few lilies blow.

And I have asked to be
    Where no storms come,
Where the green swell is in the havens dumb,
    And out of the swing of the sea.

Gerard Manley Hopkins

HEAVEN

Heaven is
The place where
Happiness is
Everywhere.

Animals
And birds sing—
As does
Everything.

To each stone,
"How-do-you-do?"
Stone answers back,
"Well! And you?"

Langston Hughes

THINGS TO REMEMBER

The buttercups in May
The wild rose on the spray
The poppy in the hay

The primrose in the dell
The freckled foxglove bell,
The honeysuckle's smell

Are things I would remember
When cheerless, raw November
Makes room for dark December.

James Reeves

Rhythm: The teacher may feel that a number of children's poems do not fit into the cyclical or dialectical image patterns. These are the rhythmic poems and chants that are analogous to the work songs and lullabies of adult poetry. Some examples follow:

LAMPLIGHTER BARN

I can play
in the prickly hay
and I can find
where the chickens lay
and take off my shoes

and stay
and stay
in the tickly hay
on a rainy day.

Myra Cohn Livingston

THE PICKETY FENCE

The pickety fence
The pickety fence
Give it a lick it's
The pickety fence
Give it a lick it's
A clickety fence
Give it a lick it's
A lickety fence
Give it a lick
Give it a lick
Give it a lick
With a rickety stick
Pickety
Pickety
Pickety
Pick.

David McCord

Poems such as these are best experienced in situations that provide opportunity for physical response: movement to the rhythms, miming the action and the rhythm, speaking the words chorally, setting them to music for singing, and the like. With such poems an active participation in their rhythms and a delight in repetitions, rhymes, and word plays for their own sake are what constitute criticism for the elementary child.

Chapter 7

The Study of Story

> One essential aspect of literary training, and one that
> it is possible to acquire, or begin acquiring, in childhood,
> is the art of listening to stories. This sounds like a passive
> ability, but it is not passive at all: it is what the army
> would call a basic training for the imagination.
>
> NORTHROP FRYE*

Discourse and Non-Discourse

In addition to experience with poetry, the young child's literary
education includes prose, particularly the prose of story rather than
of discourse. A clear line should be drawn between discursive and
non-discursive writing in the literary experience of the child. Imaginative structures should be experienced first as they are, with no
attempt to "translate" them into discursive language. In Northrop
Frye's words:

> I keep insisting on capitalizing on and exploiting a small child's
> attention when you're telling him a story, because to hold that
> attention until the story is told is a very rare mental achievement
> for an adult. Children can do it, and if you can persuade a child
> to keep on doing it, he won't have any trouble with literature.
> But, instead, children get switched over to the values of the prose
> civilization and the conception of content so that they are trained
> to look at every work of literature, or at paintings, for that matter,
> or even music, and to say: "What's in it for me?" "What can I

---

*"The Developing Imagination," *Learning in Language and Literature*, A. R. Mac-
Kinnon and Northrop Frye (Cambridge: Harvard University Press, 1963), p. 43.

grab and carry off?" They look at a poem or painting and say: "What does it mean?" "Explain it to me so I can get something out of it." But the very simple childish response of staring at a picture or being absorbed in a poem as a whole is exactly what the painter or poet wants you to do.*

Stories requiring little or no explication or commentary should be chosen and presented as entities. In listening to or reading a story as an entity the child's mind is directed toward total structure rather than snippets of content. The whole design of a literary work is comprehended only when it is experienced as a whole. Furthermore, children should be encouraged to hear a story out before questioning it. Those who may make objections to talking pigs and airborne carpets are confusing discursive and imaginative writing. Stories are to be accepted as stories. Children should be invited to hear them through, making no attempt to judge them in terms of external standards of "truth" as though they were factual or informational writing. As Coleridge suggested, we need to acquire "a willing suspension of disbelief."

A work of literature is a body of hypothetical thought and action, expressing not what happened but what *happens,* in Aristotle's sense of the typical, recurrent, universal event. Questions about literature should turn in on the literature itself, with no attempt to test its "truth" against external correspondences. We do not ask: Is it true that there is a Yellow Brick Road? but: Is it imaginatively conceivable that there could be?

Asking Literary Questions

Thus, the first act of literary criticism is a simple one. Stories are read or listened to as stories. If there are questions, they should come from the children. Even these should be guided so that children come to think of content in terms of structure and form rather than in relationship to something extraneous to the story. If the child inquires, for example, why the story ended as it did or why a character behaved in a certain way, the teacher will *take him back into the story itself to find the answer.* Irrelevant questions are those that ask, "Did the boy behave as you would?" "What would you have done had you been in his place?" and the like because their answers lead the child outside of the story and align its "meaning" with external meanings.

*Author's interview with Northrop Frye, January 12, 1970.

Content, in the discussion of literature, cannot, of course, be ignored. However, we should try to talk about content as far as possible in terms of form and structure. If, as an example, the child says: "I don't like the way the writer makes the boy behave," it might be profitable to say, "Well, write a story of your own or rewrite this one and work out his behavior to suit yourself." Such an exercise, when practical, would help the child to see that a character's behavior need not always be considered in terms of its moral implications. A character often behaves the way he does in order for the story to develop along certain lines; characters may, in fact, be examined *structurally.* To use an example from children's literature: Templeton the rat, in E. B. White's *Charlotte's Web,* may not be a thoroughly desirable character, but he serves the purpose of the plot precisely because he *is* undesirable.

Questions that begin with "Why?" are to be encouraged, because they direct the child to a consideration of the reasons the author used a particular technique. What is bad pedagogically is to make the child remember what is said in a passage. What is right pedagogically is the asking of questions like "Why did he say it in this way?" The children as critics should not be bogged down with the memorization of factual detail related to stories they read and hear. The aim is to guide them to see relationships, patterns, and analogies among many stories and literary experiences, not to transfix them in the detailed examination of a single story, even though that story is first considered as an entity.

Content is an aspect of story that cannot, of course, be divorced from form and structure, but neither should form and structure be sacrificed wholly to content. A story first and always provides pleasure or involvement for a reader-listener. It should not be used for any other purpose. Stories, good and bad, will incidentally present values and offer vicarious and perhaps broadening experience. They are, however, *story* first and foremost. Children should be discouraged from reading stories for messages and morals or miscellaneous general knowledge, however valuable all of these may be. *The Tale of Peter Rabbit,* for example, may be seen as having a very definite moral. Read one way it teaches that if you disobey your mother you may be endangered, lose your clothes, feel ill, and be sent to bed with medication. Another valid interpretation might be that disobedience means an active and exciting life. In either case, the literary point of the story is missed; for the tale of Peter is the classic adventure story of romance, with Peter, the typical hero, home triumphant—albeit a little sick to his stomach—after successfully completing a quest.

Content, then, should be discussed as far as possible in terms of form and structure. This approach facilitates many of the understandings we want to develop in beginning literary critics. If the child examines form and structure, he will become aware that stories come in a certain limited number of conventional shapes and that certain patterns of imagery are common to different types of story. He will begin to see the patterns in story: how major and minor characters relate and reveal themselves through the design of situation and incident.

Literary questions that center in form and structure are such as these:

—Did the story end as you expected it to? Did the author prepare you to expect the ending? How?

—Suppose we thought of a different ending for the story. How would the rest of the story have to be changed for the new ending?

—What does the author do to get the story going? Suppose that opening were changed or removed, how would the rest of the story be changed?

—What kind of person was the principal character? Did he apparently change during the course of the story? How? What caused him to change?

—Suppose this or that character were removed from the story. How would the whole be changed?

—Suppose the order of events were changed. What would happen to the story? Would it be a new story or no story at all?

—Where does the story take place? If it took place somewhere else or in a different time, how would it be changed?

—What does the author do to create suspense, to make you want to read on to find out what happens?

—Every story writer creates a make-believe world and peoples it with characters. Even where the world is far different from your own (as in fantasy), how does the author make his story seem possible and probable?

—What signs and signals indicate that a story will be fanciful rather than realistic? Funny rather than serious?

—In what ways is this story and its characters like others you have read, heard, or seen?

Comprehension and Response

Many teachers seem to feel that theirs are the only valid questions to be asked in the classroom. In a nervous effort to check basic comprehension of a story, or to have the children see it from *their point of view,* teachers are likely to isolate such parts of the whole as sequence of events or descriptive detail and make this the subject of questioning. Or they assign the kiss of death: the book report. Since story is quite unlike discursive writing from which specific information and facts may be extracted, it is inappropriate to test whether the child has understood a story by a series of questions that treat the story as informational writing. There are many ways to understand a story and they are *not all translatable* into descriptive prose. A more appropriate test of the child's comprehension of the stories he reads and hears is an artistic or creative response.

After a story is read, children, individually or in groups, have at their disposal a variety of creative responses. Through their dramatizations they will demonstrate whether they have grasped characterization, sequence of events, mood, and the like. Through art work related to the story, they will indicate their grasp of the same elements in addition to details about setting and the depth of their imaginative grasp of the story. Individual conferences may be scheduled with those who need specific help with the reading of story. Elizabeth Parker's *Teaching the Reading of Fiction* is a comprehensive reference teachers will find useful in providing such help.

The creative response to literature is, of course, more than a test of comprehension. It constitutes a major aspect of the entire critical process. If the child is able to act out the key scenes of a story he has heard, he is aware of the structure of that story; if he is able to make a picture of a character or scene from a book, he has been able to visualize what he has read or heard; if he is able to write an episode making use of a character in a story, he has been able to grasp the details that make up that character.

In the young child a valid critical response may be more basic than creative. He may wriggle with delight or wiggle in boredom. He may sigh or gasp or join in on a refrain. He may ask to hear the story "one more time" or go off, starry-eyed, clutching the book it was read from.

Presenting Stories to Children

The actual study of literature has traditionally been reserved for older students or elementary students who are considered to be superior readers and reasoners. If a child is a slow learner, it is commonly believed that he has only time for learning the basic communication skills and little time for anything that is not strictly utilitarian. This elitist approach to literary studies is nonsense, not to mention its being anti-humanistic. The less intellectually gifted child should not be deprived of literature while he receives extra instruction in the practical and utilitarian uses of language. Even the dullest child will profit from imaginative "basic training": he can listen to stories and poems, even though he may not be able to read them independently.

The child understands with ear and heart what may be beyond the reach of his eye as a reader. Story "reading" competency may, therefore, be developed with the youngest children and with those who are not independent readers, for stories may always be presented orally by someone who does read independently. They may also be presented through pictures such as film strips, or through films. Dramatization is yet another form of presentation for story, valued for its own sake, and because it may be used when decoding skills are absent or minimal. An oral or visual presentation, or a combination of the two, allows all pupils, whether they read independently or not, to become absorbed effortlessly in a story as a whole and so be able to grasp its total structure. An oral presentation has another factor to recommend it—it allows the children to hear the storyteller's "voice." The printed form of a story is merely an echo of that voice and must be interpreted as effectively and vividly as possible if it is to be brought fully to life. Fine stories, like poetry, are meant to be heard; their rhythms provide memorable linguistic patterns to be absorbed by the children.

Children should experience the widest possible variety of stories: myths, Bible tales told as stories, legends, tales of the heroes of epic and romance, folk and fairy tales, fables, realistic stories, fantasy, and all the rest. Story means novels, short stories, and tales; or excerpts from book-length stories or novels, if they are selected for the quality of their story within a story.

Most stories for children, until the last few years, have been comic or romantic in shape. Recently, however, realistic stories in the ironic mode dominating the adult literary scene have had an influence on children's literature. Although it is true that young children seem to respond well to the comic and romantic structures, older children of today respond equally well to ironic and, to a lesser extent, satiric parodies of these structures. There are, at any rate, elements of both tragedy and irony in children's stories beginning with Humpty Dumpty's disastrous end and the ironic comeuppances experienced by the indomitable Punch of Punch and Judy, who invariably, after triumphantly besting everyone in sight, is himself annihilated by the one enemy he failed to foil. Stories in all four of the modes, or stories that contain elements of all four modes, should be included in a well-balanced curriculum for today's children, if their elementary experience is to prepare them adequately for literary encounters at more sophisticated levels by making them as insightful as they can be *right now.*

All through the elementary school a student should become gradually aware that stories come in certain conventional shapes. As he becomes familiar with a variety of stories, even the youngest child notes formal similarities among them. He anticipates events: "The 'good guy' will catch the 'bad guy' 'cause 'good guys' always win." He learns to predict outcomes by sizing up beginnings: "It starts 'Once upon a time' so it's a 'lived-happily-ever-after' story." "It starts with trouble but it looks like the hero can solve the problem so it will end happy." With experience of stories he learns to distinguish "Believe" from "Make-Believe" by their very different qualities.

The fundamental literary patterns and conventions derived from myth and ritual are best seen in literature like the epic, the saga, and the fairy tale. In the traditional narrative a king or hero goes forth to engage in a contest or combat, his story clearly illustrating a pattern basic to literature, the quest. Vestiges of the ancient myths and rituals persist in traditional stories. Legends, epics, fairy tales, and the like are concerned primarily with supernatural beings, kings, and heroes, as were the rituals that gave birth to them. In ritual drama it was common for a man, disguised as an animal, to speak or to suddenly remove his animal disguise and appear as himself. Storytellers are steeped in story, their stories growing out of other stories consciously and unconsciously. The quest as a plot design, characters like kings and heroes, conventions like transformations and talking animals recur in tales that provide readers and hearers with a sense of the venerability of story structure and convention. Traditional literature is to literature what still life is to painting: studies in basic form. The old tales form a basis for evaluating the structure of all subsequent stories.

The traditional stories of a culture also put the child in contact with many of the "social myths" that have figured in the development of his society. Every society has a central group of stories that inform not only its literature but other aspects of its social life as well. The major myths explain the origin of social classes; they account for rituals and the like. A knowledge of them through literature can make social life more intelligible. Literary works that express these informing social myths most clearly are works that should receive the educator's attention, whenever it is possible to use them. They are not invariably the books of greatest literary value. Included among them are stories of the Horatio Alger type, celebrating virtuous behavior and enterprise as means to financial and social success, and stories that contain more modern "myths" as they show the tuned-out or turned-off youth seeking value within himself as he rejects the value systems of his parents.

The child's literary experience includes the old and new, the "bad" and "good," the stories encountered in school and those encountered out of it. A "good" story is a well-constructed story, since the problems the artist has in beginning, developing, and concluding his story are problems that will exist as long as stories are told.

The question of what is morally suitable or unsuitable for children's consumption is inappropriate for consideration here, except to say that it is virtually impossible to protect children entirely from stories whose content, from an adult viewpoint, is undesirable for them. Questions of desirability usually turn on matters of content rather than structure. If children were to consider story *first* *as story* in school and direct their attention to structure and form *before* content, they might well be developing an immunity to the effects of unwholesomeness in stories. Certainly, if their critical endeavors are centered in a consideration of form and structure, they will be able to evaluate all of the stories they encounter. They will learn for themselves how certain movies, television dramas, and children's serials in book form are weak structurally— predictable, lacking in character motivation, making use of heavy manipulation of incident for effect. Both the mediocre and excellent are part of the child's literary experience, for almost all children watch television, read comics, and delight in series books at one time or another, and it is to be hoped that their school experience would provide them with some of the best possible literary encounters. It is only through wide exposure to the best, the mediocre, and the worst that the child will eventually develop taste and judgment as well as critical astuteness.

It is important that the child have as mixed a bag as possible, folk tales and the like, modern realistic stories, and fantasy. Modern stories are essentially "displacements" of the basic story patterns. The Cinderella story, for example, is in the comic mode: the archetypal pattern for the very latest "success story" with its sudden reversal of fortune that culminates, often miraculously, in a happy ending. Because they employ the pattern of the successful quest of the hero, the Old Testament story of David's triumph over Goliath and the modern picture book that shows a little boy coping with the modern "giants" of his experience are in the same romantic mode.

The young literary critic reads and hears a wide variety of stories as stories. This is the first step along the critical path. Avoiding personal value judgments and abstract analysis, criticism for children is centered in imaginative response; within a deductive framework supplied by the teacher, the child works inductively to make analogies, note resemblances, and relate all aspects of his literary experience from folk tales to modern novels.

Since the best of literature is not written with a controlled vocabulary or with particular attention to length or structure of sentences, the age-grade label attached to many stories may safely be removed. Where children cannot read the stories for themselves, the teacher can read aloud to them. As a professional aware of the needs and the level of ability of a particular class, the teacher will make choices in accordance with his pupils' best interests, always bearing in mind that it is his responsibility to foster new interests and broaden literary experience.

Obviously some stories, because of their content, length, and structure, are eminently more suited for use with kindergarten to third grade than others: nursery tales like "The Three Bears," "The Three Pigs," "Henny Penny," and "The Gingerbread Boy"; and picture story books with their simple vocabularly and repetitive patterns, such as Wanda Gág's *Millions of Cats,* Barbara Emberley's *Drummer Hoff,* and Harve Zemach's *The Judge.* Folk and fairy tales, tales of the heroes of epic and romance, and book-length stories are for grades four to six. But the designation of grade level in the case of literature can never be rigidly adhered to. Little children, for instance, will readily grasp a telling or reading of a simple version of the Moses story, while a more complex version of the tale, with the text taken from the Bible, would be reserved for older children.

Archetypal criticism, with its look at the broad patterns in literature, does not limit the teacher to a list of stories by grade, a classification that is always arbitrary and restricting. A good story bears a second or even third retelling, as all teachers, librarians, and parents well know. Stories children have read or encountered in some form in other years will form part of their critical discussions. The cry of "We've had this before" is to be welcomed rather than feared and avoided, for former exposure can be turned to good use when children are considering stories not merely as separate entities, but as parts of the whole universe of story and poetry. They will be encouraged to review or remember stories encountered earlier for the sake of comparison: to note similarities of structural patterns, to see how the same type of character turns up again and again, to note recurrent patterns of imagery and symbolism.

Archetypal Literary Criticism Applied to Story

The practice of archetypal criticism involves a stepping back from the individual poem or story to see it in the context of literature as a whole, as one of a family of stories and poems: a literary universe. It is taken for granted that the archetypal critic has mastered the story-reading abilities appropriate to his level of maturity. He can listen to a story all the way through, holding in his mind sequence of events, relationships among characters, and significant detail; he is able to make inferences and predict outcomes; he is alert to nuances in tone and mood. These and other basic abilities in story reading are developed progressively as each new story is encountered in the classroom. In addition, the teacher structures learning sequences that allow the children to consider individual stories in relationship to others and as part of the whole universe of literature. Simulations of the discussion portions of a number of learning sequences are presented on the following pages as examples. They show how basic critical understandings may be fostered by a process of inductive reasoning.

The Quest of the Hero

Children should progressively develop a sense of the "one story" of all literature: the story of the loss and regaining of identity. This "story" is exemplified in the quest of the mythical hero whose adventures, death, disappearance, and return become the four generic plots of literature: romance, tragedy, irony-satire, and comedy.

Children should experience the hero stories in versions appropriate to their level of understanding. Younger children, for example, might be told aloud the story of David and Goliath; older students might be expected to read the same story themselves from the scriptures or a collection of Bible stories.

The hero stories of all cultures would be included in learning sequences, for variety and for the sake of comparison. Besides the hero tales of the Judaeo-Christian tradition, there are the Greek tales of Perseus, Theseus, and Hercules. There is the ancient epic of Gilgamesh, written in cuneiform five thousand years ago, that tells of a Sumerian king who undertook a long, dangerous journey in a search for immortality. There is the English epic of Beowulf and the tale of King Arthur, and the traditional French and German stories of Roland and Siegfried.

The concept of the quest of the hero offers numerous possibilities for critical analysis. A comparison of hero tales from many lands will reveal similarities in story form and structure: in most stories, for instance, a mystery surrounds the hero's birth. The *pattern* of the hero story will become evident to them as children read or listen to numbers of these tales. Comparison of the hero of the traditional tale with the hero or principal character of modern fiction is inevitable. Children may be led to an understanding of how all such stories, old and new, are alike in form and structure although their content may differ dramatically. Each story is in its way the story of a search for identity. Even in modern tales the young hero is likely to undergo a series of trials that often include a climactic adventure, and in many cases a kind of ritual death, a story pattern that reaches back to myth. In modern realistic fiction the hero has very different powers of action than has the hero of myth and romance; as they gain familiarity with all types of hero stories, children will be able to see these differences for themselves.

In reading and discussing the characteristics of the hero—ancient and modern—children may be led to an understanding of how the story of the hero's quest connects with the two opposite poles of man's imagination. The hero, as he works to restore a lost perfection or harmony or to gain recognition or identity, is very likely someone with whom we would like to identify; his enemies and the negative aspects of his environment, on the other hand, represent our fears and nightmares or what we would like to avoid.

Character Conventions

Children should begin to understand that certain types of characters are common to certain types of stories, that the same *type* of character keeps turning up in different forms in all kinds of stories.

Exposure to hero stories and discussion of the concept of the hero in fiction will be one way to illustrate the principle of recurrent character types. Typical character types other than the hero may be isolated for examination: the evil goddess of the myth is related to the witch of the romance, to the evil stepmother of the fairy tale, and to the impossible female parent as depicted in a number of modern ironic stories for children. The helpful goddess of myth becomes the kindly sorceress of romance, the fairy godmother of the fairy tale, and the kindly mother figure of the modern realistic story.

Children will be able to see what basic types of characters are associated with the hero's quest and which basic types are against it. They will note that there are neutral, flat, or static characters in many stories who add little to the action but who have other functions: to make the hero look more heroic, to make him appear more handsome, or more clever, to give him assistance, to be his "straight man."

Children should not be required to make moral judgments about the characters they encounter. They should be helped to see that characters of all kinds are needed as *structural principles* in story. In *The 500 Hats of Bartholomew Cubbins,* for instance, the role of villain is served by the Grand Duke Wilfred, nephew to the king, who is portrayed as sadistically cruel, haughty, and contemptuous. His characteristics are certainly not those that a conscientious teacher hopes young readers will emulate. However, it would be unfortunate to moralize about Wilfred's behavior in an effort to influence children not to behave as he does. Wilfred is central to the structure of the story. His sadistic interest in permanently getting rid of both Bartholomew *and* his hats leads the hero into dangerous and suspenseful situations that culminate in the climax of the story, where the duke is about to push Bartholomew from a parapet to his death. The fact that Bartholomew's adversaries now include a boy his own age, but his opposite in character and social status, provides by means of contrast and comparison an added dimension to the conflict. Not only does Wilfred move the plot forward, but his actions also move it into added excitement and suspense; rather than censuring his nastiness, readers should consider what the story would be like without the evil Wilfred, and gain more literary profit in the process.

Cyclical and Dialectical Imagery

Experience with both poetry and story, if the teacher structures learning sequences designed to foster insights, can lead the children to an understanding of the two structures that underlie literary imagery. The cyclical pattern is exemplified in the association of certain seasons and times of year with particular stories or parts of stories. Beginnings and quests, for instance, are likely to take place in the "merry months" of May and June, as in the old ballads. Endings and failures are often associated with the "death" of the year: fall and winter. Triumph, the full powers of the hero, and the like are most often associated with spring and summer.

A dialectical structure also underlies literary imagery. Man's dreams and visions are associated with gardens and paradises; his nightmares with deserts, threatening forests, and wastelands. As man seeks in his literature to identify with a neutral nature, he uses certain natural settings to reflect atmosphere and mood. Some colors are associated with dreams, others with nightmares. Black and grey are most often the colors of the sinister, for example; gold and white, of the noble and pure. (It may be pointed out that this has no relation whatsoever to race. It is probable that dark colors are sinister because the darkness of night terrified man; the gold of the sun warmed him.) The unicorn, lamb, and dove—peaceful animals and birds—are friends of the hero of romance, to use another example; but the serpent and the raven typically belong with the dark powers that oppose him.

As they read both poetry and story, children should be led toward an understanding of the kind of language employed in literature. The literary imagination has always sought to suggest an identity between the human mind and the world outside it. It does so by means of metaphor, the language of identification: "This is that." This process of identification or association, by means of words, began with early man's identification with animals, plants, and the forces of nature when he created stories that featured man-like gods who were associated with the sun, the sea, and other natural objects and phenomena. The process continues from mythology and is the very essence of literary expression.

Structuring Learning Sequences with Story: Five Examples

Though actual classroom discussion will seldom be as "perfect" as the simulated discussions given below, they are included to illustrate how the basic critical understandings just described may be fostered through careful questioning. The teacher may select specific stories for presentation that exemplify the particular understanding he wants to develop. However, children are encouraged, in the course of the discussion, to call upon *all* of their literary experiences where they apply to the subject under consideration.

I. Aim of the sequence: To lead children in the primary grades of elementary school toward an understanding that stories come in certain conventional "shapes."

Discussion:

Teacher: We have read *Little Tim and the Brave Sea Captain, Where the Wild Things Are,* and *The Tale of Peter Rabbit.* They are all stories about very different things, it's true, but can you think of any ways the stories are alike?

Pupils: —Tim and Peter and Max all do exciting things.

—They all get into danger.

—They leave home and go far away.

—And have great adventures.

—Lots of things happen to them.

—But they all get home okay at the end.

—Everything ends happy, except Peter feels sick.

—But he did okay; he got away from the man who was chasing him.

—Max didn't really go away; it was just a dream.

—It's the same thing, though. He went away in his mind.

Teacher: Could you say that the stories are shaped like this? *(He draws a circle on the board.)*

Pupils: —Yeah. They all end up where they started.

—Max goes away and has a trip and comes back to his room.

—Peter runs away from his house and gets into trouble in the garden and comes back home at the end.

—So does Tim.

Teacher: Do you know any other stories that have that same shape?

Pupils: —In "The Three Billy Goats Gruff" they don't come back to any place, but they end up safe at the end. Is that the same thing?

—Sure. It's the same way with lots of stories. Bad things happen all the way through, but things turn out okay at the end.

—That's the way it always is. Even in westerns. The good guy ends up okay even though he nearly gets killed.

—I know one story where that doesn't happen: the Gingerbread Boy doesn't get away safe at the end. He gets eaten.

—That doesn't happen very often in stories, though.

—Most of them are circles. They end up with things okay, just the way they started.

II. Aim of the sequence: To help older children to the understanding that the hero story relates to the dialectical structure of literary imagery. The hero's quest involves his effort to regain a lost identity, to restore harmony or perfection.

Discussion:

Teacher: What does the hero most often do in these stories?

Pupils: —He goes looking for something, like Sir Lancelot looking for the Holy Grail.

—Or Jason after the Golden Fleece.

—He goes to capture an enemy or get rid of something horrible.

—Right. Perseus was trying to kill that monster Medusa.

—Sometimes he acts on a challenge or dare.

—Hercules had to do twelve labors as a punishment for committing a murder.

—Sometimes the guy goes to do something because he's really unhappy about the way things are where he is and he wants to change them.

—I guess you could say Moses did that.

—Never mind Moses. Marshal Dillon in *Gunsmoke* does the same thing.

—Does that count? He's not one of these old heroes.

—He's still supposed to be a hero.

—Some heroes just go to seek their fortunes, like some of those types in fairy tales. You're always getting

youngest sons who leave home to try and make it big.
—The hero is always looking for something good or for
something better. He seems to be looking for *something*.
—Something good. A hero story always has some kind
of search in it.

Teacher: Is that true of heroes and heroines in modern stories
that we've read? Take *Call It Courage,* for an example.
Pupils: —Sure. That kid is searching for something. He's trying
to find his own courage, I guess you could say.
—And the guy in *The Loner* is looking for something, too.
I'm not sure exactly what or if he even knows at the
beginning.
—Sure he does. He doesn't like the life he has to lead.
He tries to find something better. It's still a search.
—They're all the same, these heroes. They have a dream
that they want to make come true.

III. Aim of the sequence: To help older children gain an understanding of the cyclical structure that underlies literary imagery.

Discussion:

Teacher: If you were to write about something unpleasant or sad,
what season of the year would you be likely to have
it take place in?
Pupils: —Probably in the fall when things are dying.
—Or in the winter when they're dead.

Teacher: And if you were writing a happy story?
Pupils: —It could be in the winter, if you liked snow and stuff.
Winter and fall.
—That's not the point. In most stories good things are
put with good weather.
—I don't agree.

Teacher: Suppose we think of it in another way. *(Draws a circle
on the chalkboard and labels each of its parts: summer,
spring, fall, and winter, respectively.)* Let's see if this
makes any sense according to the stories we know.
First, what happens in the spring and summer in nature?

Pupils: —Things start growing.
　　　　　—Everything is alive.
　　　　　—Everything is green and new and fresh.
Teacher: What happens in fall and winter to natural things?
Pupils: —They die.
　　　　　—Or go to sleep under the snow; seeds, I mean.

Teacher: Now, can you think of any stories you know that are
　　　　　spring stories, *even though they don't mention that time
　　　　　of year?*
Pupil: —You mean where stories are like the seasons, in a way.
Teacher: That's right.
Pupils: —Well, I guess you could say that "The Sleeping Beauty"
　　　　　begins as a winter story and ends as spring.
　　　　　—So does "Beauty and the Beast."
　　　　　—And "Cinderella."
　　　　　—And "The Ugly Duckling!"
　　　　　—And even *Charlie and the Chocolate Factory.*
　　　　　—*Charlotte's Web,* too.
　　　　　—Practically all stories for that matter go from bad to
　　　　　good at the end, sort of.
　　　　　—Right! In *Charlotte's Web* they're all set to kill Wilbur
　　　　　at the beginning, but he's safe at the end.
　　　　　—Most stories I've read or heard of are like that. They
　　　　　start out peaceful for a while, then everything gets
　　　　　scary and dangerous, maybe, but it all ends up okay.
　　　　　—So, it's something like a circle, like the seasons in a
　　　　　way, I guess: summer, fall, or winter, then spring again.

Teacher: There's another way we might look at this. We said
　　　　　that spring was a time when natural things were just
　　　　　beginning to grow, and summer when they have grown
　　　　　and developed. What stories do you know that are
　　　　　"spring" stories, where the hero is just beginning to
　　　　　grow?
Pupil: —You mean to get bigger?

Teacher: Well, partly, but it could also mean to grow up. What
　　　　　does it mean to grow up?
Pupils: —You start to learn things.
　　　　　—Things happen to you to give you experiences you
　　　　　haven't had before. Is that what you mean?

Teacher: Yes. Are there any stories like that?

Pupils: —Sure. *Rufus M.* is one. Rufus is starting to grow up.

—Manolo in *Shadow of a Bull* grows up when he decides that he knows best about his own future.

—The guy in *The Flight of the Doves* grows up; he has to, to take care of his sister.

—Mafatu in *Call It Courage* grows up fast. He has to learn to take care of himself.

—It's the same with the boy in *Dorp Dead.*

—In most stories people learn things about people and what happens in life.

—And they learn about themselves. Mafatu learned that he really did have the courage to fight the sea.

Teacher: Could you say that those are seasonal stories?

Pupil: —You could compare them to the seasons, I guess; to spring and summer, maybe.

Teacher: This is harder: do you know any autumn or winter stories?

Pupils: —*The Jazz Man,* maybe. That's a sad story. The kid suffers a lot and things don't get much better for him at the end.

—The Norse myth we read, "The Death of Balder," is a winter story; Balder is dead at the end.

—But even there it says that he's going to a place after he dies where it's always summer.

—*Sounder* is an autumn and winter story, but even there you get the idea that there's some hope. Things won't always be so bad for the boy.

—Maybe. But even so at the end his family still has a pretty bleak future in a lot of ways.

—A wintry future!

IV. Aim of the sequence: To bring children toward an understanding of the dialectical structure that underlies patterns of literary imagery.

Discussion:

Teacher: Let's try out a game like "Twenty Questions" on some of the stories we know. The categories of the game are animal, vegetable, and mineral. Now suppose the story is a happy one, what animals would be likely to be associated with it?

Pupils: —I've never thought of it before, but I guess it would be gentle animals, you know, animals that are used to being with people, like the horse in *The Goose Girl.*

—Cats are usually on the good guy's side. Dick Whittington had a cat.

—Puss in Boots helped his master out.

—Pigs are often heroes themselves; like Padre Porko!

—Or Wilbur in *Charlotte's Web.*

—Wolves and foxes, things like that, are usually the "bad guys," always playing tricks and trying to eat up the hero.

—Like in "The Three Little Pigs."

—And "Little Red Riding Hood."

—And in "Henny Penny."

Teacher: All right. Now, think of the natural surroundings in stories that tell about happy things. What kind of plants are there in those, usually? What does the countryside look like?

Pupils: —When everything's okay and things are going fine for the hero, he's usually in a nice place, comfortable, like his own house, maybe.

—But when he's in trouble, things usually look pretty gloomy with lots of rocks and no trees.

—Like Perseus. The place where he was looking for Medusa was all grey with no sun ever shining there.

—And Rapunzel was banished to a dark wood and then to a place like a desert.

—Yeah, but when the prince found her again, they went to a neat palace where everything looked nice.

—Practically all stories are like that, I guess. Writers put all the good things together.

—Things around you sort of match the way you feel.

—Well, anyway, they do in stories.

V. Aim of the sequence: To lead children to an awareness of the dialectic structure that underlies literary imagery, man's two dreams as expressed in his literature. At one limit of his desire is the wasteland or wilderness; at the other is his vision of a garden or paradise.

Discussion:

Teacher: Most people daydream, I think. I know a few people right here who do. I do myself. What exactly is a daydream?

Pupils: —If you're bored, or mad, or something, you just think of a better place to be and go there in your mind.

—You make up something in your mind that takes you away from where you are. You take a trip!

—In your head.

Teacher: We talk about daydreams but not about day-nightmares. Why is that?

Pupil: —Most daydreams are about things you want or wish you could do; they're not about horrible things that you want to get away from. Nightmares are.

Teacher: Have you ever thought that stories show both kinds of dreams, pleasant dreams and nightmares?

Pupils: —Almost all stories are about making some dream or wish come true.

—People want a better life, maybe, and they try to make what they want happen.

Teacher: What stories do you know that are like that? Start by thinking of the myths and hero tales we have read.

Pupils: —Moses wanted to lead the children of Israel to where they wouldn't be slaves any longer.

—Prometheus wanted to give fire to man so he could live a better life, one more like the gods.

—Gilgamesh wanted to find a place where people were always young and there was no death.

Teacher: Are there any newer stories that show the same thing?

Pupils: —The biography of Harriet Tubman. She was leading slaves out of captivity, like Moses.

—Stories about pioneers show them working hard to make their surroundings more civilized and fit to live in. The *Little House* books tell all about that.

—In *Journey Outside* the boy is tired of his life with the Raft People who always talk about finding a better place to live but don't do anything about it. Dilar goes himself and finds something better. He wants his grandfather and the others to share it with him.

Teacher: Do people in books always succeed in making their dreams come true?

Pupils: —Not always. It's a sad story when they don't, though.

—But that's the way things are in real life. You can't always get what you want. Too many stories are phoney. Somebody wants to get something or do something and no matter what, but it always works out okay at the end and he gets what he was after. In a lot of stories, like the ones on TV, you know beforehand that whatever the person wants he'll get. It's phoney.

—Maybe it is, but there wouldn't be any story if the person in it wasn't trying to get something or do something, would there?

—Well, he doesn't always have to get his own way. That's not the way things are in life.

—Right. But we're talking about stories, and most stories end up with *something* happening that the hero or whoever wanted to have happen at the beginning.

—Sometimes it's not exactly like making a dream come true, but things are better at the end than they were at the beginning. In *It's Like This, Cat,* the kid didn't have any big dreams come true, but at least at the end of the story he felt a little better about his family and everything.

—Right. You could say that dreams go in both directions: up and down!

Structuring Additional Learning Sequences with Story

Classification and Categorization

It will help children become aware of recurrent structures and patterns and themes if they try to classify what they read in different ways. Many stories will fit into more than one category. Categories may be evolved with the children or supplied by the teacher. Stories may be classified in any of the following ways:

—By their "shapes": comic, romantic, tragic, ironic. The characteristics of each story "shape" are elicited from the children after experience with all kinds of stories.

—According to seasonal cycles: some stories are "spring" and "summer" stories where the hero is young and comes to maturity and his full powers; some are "autumn" or "winter" stories where the hero dies, does not realize his quest, or fails to complete it; where he loses his strength or even his life.

—According to the dialectic pattern: stories may show the world man wants and the world he rejects; often one story can handle the struggle between these two opposites. Some stories show the realization of the goals man seeks; others show his failure to "lift himself up," showing bitterness and defeat.

—Stories may be classified in a number of other ways, the sophistication of the classifications varying in accordance with the ability of grades and classes within grades:
   (a) stories that end happily or sadly
   (b) stories of successful quests
   (c) stories of wish-fulfillment
   (d) stories of dreams and stories of nightmares
The categories are supplied by the teacher as well as by a number of the stories, but the examples are drawn from all aspects of the children's literary and sub-literary experience. They will find, for instance, examples of the wish-fulfillment story not only in classic tales like "Cinderella," but also in many television commercials and serials as well as films.

—Another way to classify stories is by considering them according to the hero's power of action: whether it is greater than ours, less, or much the same. The categories might be provided for the children, with them working in groups to classify the stories they know. Comic and cartoon characters should be included: Superman is like a god, Charlie Brown is an ordinary chap, Dark Shadows is like a beast or demon.

Other Learning Activities

Reading and listening to stories, asking questions about them, and answering questions and offering ideas about them in guided discussion will form the greater part of the critical process in the elementary classroom. Children should seldom if ever be asked to write answers to the literary questions they discuss. To help the children consolidate their understandings, the following types of activities, for example, are useful:

—Working in groups to make collections of stories that show the cyclical nature of poetic imagery: "spring" stories are in the comic mode, "summer" stories are in the romantic mode, "fall" stories are in the tragic mode, "winter" stories are in the ironic-satiric mode. The concept of the seasons will be offered purely as a thought construct for the examination of stories. The stories *need not deal with the seasons specifically.*

—The children can play a game similar to "Twenty Questions" with literary imagery, deciding what representatives of the animal, vegetable, and mineral world are associated with different parts of and types of stories and in what way they are associated.

—The students might create color wheels or charts to show the symbolic association of color with man's dreams and the world he rejects. It is interesting to note that a positive or negative symbolism may be associated with a color. In one context, for example, red may signify courage and fervor, in another, violence and revolt.

—Students might "collect" examples of typical characters, plots, and devices (archetypes) from comics, television, advertising, and films. Examples: the detergent that fights dirt as the knight fights evil or the magical transformations and images of paradise in other commercials.

—Picture essays could be developed showing images of desirable and undesirable worlds: straight roads or paths and mazes, trees in bloom and rows of telephone poles, domesticated animals and beasts of prey or monsters, homes and prisons, gardens and wastelands, productive people and derelicts, gentle waterfalls and destructive floods, human compassion and human cruelty.

Once a teacher understands that all literature is linked together by means of common elements that recur continually, it will be easy to think of ways to help children see connections between their literary, personal, and cultural lives. The character-types, events, stories, images, and themes that appear and reappear in literature are present in music, art, television, movies, games, current events, advertising, comics, and cartoons. Discovering these elements and making connections among them gives an added dimension to the enjoyment of individual poems and stories. Literature adds up to an exciting whole. Its influence is recognized as widespread and timeless. Man's imaginative expressions are as old as the first story and as new as each young critic's imaginative response to it.

Teaching structural principles is teaching how literature works and what it is. It is not only separate works that may be admired or despised but a unified imaginative structure of archetypal themes, conventional images and forms. There is intellectual excitement in discovering what literature is and increased imaginative power in the discovery.

Chapter 8

Composing Poetry and Story

Young people should certainly be encouraged to write, for everyone can learn to write poetry up to a point—the point of discovering how difficult it is to write it unusually well. To get to that point is no mean achievement, as it is well past the substandard level of naive or doggerel verse which is the usual mode of amateur expression. But the purpose of such encouragement is to breed a love of poetry, not to breed poets.

NORTHROP FRYE*

Poetic Composition: An Aspect of the Critical Process

Literature grows out of other literature, and experience with poetry is the best way to foster its creation. The children in the elementary school should hear poetry in quantity, they should speak it themselves, ask questions of each other and the teacher, compare and contrast different kinds and types of poems and poetic techniques, and they should in freedom be allowed to experiment with poetic creations of their own.

The poet Kenneth Koch, acting on the assumption that children are natural poets, went into a number of classrooms to teach children that they could make poems out of the expression of their "wishes, lies, and dreams." He found it most important to take "children seriously as poets. Children have a natural talent for writing

*"Poetry," *University of Toronto Quarterly*, vol. xxvi (April 1956), p. 290.

poetry and anyone who teaches them should know that. Teaching really is not the right word for what takes place: it is more like permitting the children to discover something they already have."*

When education for literacy is begun by developing and releasing "something they already have," children are likely to respond with the energy, enthusiasm, and creativity that Koch describes in his book. Since poetry is a part of their natural expression, the use of it is essential in an education that aims to develop literacy.

Input for Writing: Exposure to Forms

Writing according to a form is both a discipline and a freedom. The young poet is helped in his composition if he is provided with a pattern, as Kenneth Koch demonstrated when he had his young fellow-poets create according to formulae, either suggested by him or evolved by the children in collaboration with him. There are numerous forms that provide simple enough patterns for the expression of the children's own thoughts, experiences, wishes, dreams, and desires.

Riddles and Conundrums

We have already discussed how experience with these forms can lead naturally into the creation of original riddles, even with the very young. First lines for original works may be supplied by the teacher or contributed by class members. It may be profitable to work out one or two examples as a cooperative effort, the inspired sparking the uninspired. The creation of original riddles will help the child to see ordinary objects in new ways and to create fresh metaphors to describe them, an essential aspect of the poetic experience.

Unrhymed Forms

Rhythmic repetitions. The child's natural propensity for repetitive patterns should be indulged. The vivid images of Hilda Conkling's "I Am" might serve as a pattern for original verse:

> I am willowy boughs
> For coolness;
> I am gold-finch wings

*Kenneth Koch, *Wishes, Lies and Dreams* (New York: Chelsea House, 1970) p. 25.

For darkness;
I am a little grape
Thinking of September
I am a very small violet
Thinking of May.

For older children the sonorous repetitive rhythms of the Bible might supply a pattern:

PSALM 150

Praise ye the Lord.
Praise God in his sanctuary:
Praise him in the firmament of his power.
Praise him for his mighty acts:
Praise him according to his excellent greatness.
Praise him with the sound of the trumpet:
Praise him with the psaltery and harp.
Praise him with the timbrel and dance:
Praise him with stringed instruments and organs.
Praise him upon the loud cymbals:
Praise him upon the high sounding cymbals.
Let everything that has breath praise the Lord.
Praise ye the Lord.

Catalogue verse. Catalogue verse is as old as Homer. Vivid imagery, the basic stuff of poetry, is the heart of catalogue verse. There is no need to struggle for rhyme. An entire class may participate, the younger children dictating their ideas on a common subject while the teacher transcribes, arranging the lines in different lengths for maximum rhythmic appeal. After priming minds with a poem or two read aloud, the teacher mentions a favorite theme and the children, in a brainstorming session, call out their associations related to it, trying to express as many sensory reactions as possible. The theme might be the school itself; the poem grows with items like these: "the whirr of the pencil sharpener," "the woolly smell of damp coats drying on a winter afternoon," "songs off-key," "dusty taste of chewed pencils."

Older children working in small groups or individually create their own expressive word pictures. Rupert Brook's "The Great Lover" was the stimulus material for these lines:

These I have loved:
    Sunlight on a silken cat's back

Clear June days
White sails like birds in flight over the bay
Green trees flecked with bits of blossom
And the icy touch of water as I dive.

The biblical litany uses parallel arrangements of words and ideas in poetic patterns, the arrangement of the lines providing a rhythmic sweep when the whole is read aloud. A holiday or a holy day could be the stimulation for such a poem, the teacher supplying the starting phrase, the children the rest, the whole transcribed for maximum rhythmic flow:

Let us always be thankful
    for

        _____

        _____

        _____

        _____

    for

        _____

        _____

        _____

Haiku and tanka. An ancient Japanese form of poetry is the haiku, which, in effect, is an image created within a set form of 17 syllables. A means of expressing deep emotion, it evokes more than it states: a haiku is a miniature lyric. Older children may delight in the discipline of strict adherence to the syllabic structure, but such adherence is not the important thing. More important is the expression of an idea or feeling, caught and recorded with vividness and precision:

Hovering over us
The sky surrounds the world
Invented by God.

The tanka is the same as the haiku, with the addition of two seven-syllable lines at the end. It offers the means, for some children, of developing a thought more fully than they are able to do in the haiku, which is in essence a moment captured.

Cinquain. The cinquain also deals in pure imagery. It is an arrangement of five lines of two, four, six, eight, and two syllables, respectively. Line 1 states the title, line 2 describes the title, line

3 expresses an action, line 4 expresses a feeling, and line 5 gives another word or words for the title.

Rhymed Forms

Limericks. Nonsense verse is a particular delight for children and may be profitably used to reintroduce the joys of verse to older children who are skeptical of poetry or disenchanted as a result of negative experiences with it. Children enjoy the bounce and speed of the limerick, recognizing with smiles its suitability to humorous subjects, and easily following its rhythmic pattern by tapping it out. There are many thousands of excellent examples, like this particularly playful one by Edward Lear:

> There was an old person of Ware,
> Who rode on the back of a bear:
> When they asked, "Does it trot?" he said
> "Certainly not!
> He's a Moppsikon, Floppsikon bear!"

Couplets, tercets, and quatrains. Rhyme is an aspect of poetry that should not be stressed in children's writing of poetry. The creation of telling, vivid, fresh images is a more poetic endeavor. But children are intrigued by rhyme, and many of the poems written for them are rhymed. Reading couplets aloud and letting children supply the rhyming word is enjoyable ear training, for example:

> The world is so full of a number of things,
> I'm sure we should all be as happy as ——.

Supplying a first line and asking for a second is often a fruitful way to get young poets started.

Tercets are three-line units that may rhyme in two lines or all three, for example:

THE PEOPLE

> The ants are walking under the ground,
> And the pigeons are flying over the steeple,
> And in between are the people.

> *Elizabeth Madox Roberts*

Quatrains are four-line stanzas with a possibility of a number of rhyme schemes: aabb, abab, abcb. The rhythm of the quatrain is easy to tap out for it is regular and even:

THE TOASTER

A silver-scaled Dragon with jaws flaming red
Sits at my elbow and toasts my bread.
I hand him fat slices, and then, one by one,
He hands them back when he sees they are done.

William Jay Smith

The class or a group within it may choose a common subject for their couplets, tercets, and quatrains, putting them all together at the end to make one long poem. Common topics may be descriptions of classmates, each person's impression of a common experience, or each individual effort an expression of a wish or hope.

Ballads. Ballads, particularly the old ones, employ a cinematic technique, the pictures flashing into the reader's mind as a result of the action described; ballads contain little exposition. But there is springy rhythm and rhyme, and often a refrain, as in "Robin Hood Rescuing the Widow's Three Sons":

Now Robin Hood is to Nottingham gone,
With a link and a down, and a day.
And there he met a silly old woman,
Was weeping on the way.

A story they have read, an incident from current events or history might serve as a topic for classroom balladeers working with partners or in small groups. The ballad pattern and its variations should be firmly in mind before composing begins as a result of considerable exposure to it by ear, for younger students; by ear and eye for those who can read independently.

Literary ballads and story-poems like those of Alfred Noyes are often imagistic and vividly descriptive as well as rhythmic and repetitive. Some of these will be included with the old ballads because they are effective and for purposes of comparison. Folk songs, sea chanties, work songs, cowboy songs, spirituals, and the like are similar to the old ballads in that they express the lore of the common folk. The use of all such forms provides numerous opportunities for writing: new words for old tunes, modern work songs set to the rhythms of the old, original lullabies that follow an old form, personal or group experiences ordered in the story form of the old ballad.

"Prose" into "Poetry"

Since the young child does not speak prose and is likely to write it haltingly and inaccurately, if at all, the teacher, confronted with his garbled manuscript, is likely to despair. Major surgery is required to turn what he finds there into acceptable prose. Suppose, however, when confronted with a jumbled paragraph about a pet, he restrains the correcting pencil and, instead, transcribes this:

> my dog my dog is. black with white. One black paw, the others white my dog is noisyHe barks a lot and he wags a lot. And he eats a lot. My dog is My Best Friend. We Run. We play and we have fun.

into this:

> My Dog
> My dog is
> Black with white
> One black paw
> The others white,
> My dog is
> Noisy
> He barks
> A lot
> He wags
> A lot
> He eats
> A lot.
> My dog is
> My Best Friend
> We run
> We play
> We have fun!

An imaginative and sympathetic treatment transforms what is in prose unnecessary repetition into an element of poetry, respects the child's natural expression, and offers him the encouragement needed to undertake more ambitious literary endeavors.

Poetic patterns may also be created by the alert teacher from the children's conversation, these "poems" used both as classroom reading material and as illustrations of how words may be ordered in poetic patterns. Such experiments will offer proof to the teacher of the children's natural propensity for repetition and the rhythmic use of language in their natural expression. A teacher, for example, might join a small group of kindergartners or first graders to share their talk about a recent visit to the zoo. Transcribed on his note pad or on an experience chart, their conversation might look like this:

> *Teacher:* What did you see at the zoo?
> *Pupils:* A lion, a lion, I saw a lion.
>   Monkeys, I saw monkeys, lots of monkeys.
>   I saw a tiny, tiny elephant.
>   I saw a big baboon.
>   A *big* baboon!
>   At the zoo . . . at the zoo I saw a hippo,
>   A huge old hippo.
>   At the zoo . . .

Composing involves an ordering of experience in words. The emphasis is upon experimentation with all of the forms that poets have used to order experience. Composition may be oral or written but the children's literary efforts are always undertaken in the context of other literature, for literature is *created* out of other literature.

Composing Story: Part of the Process of Literary Criticism

Composing is an important aspect of the critical experience. A knowledge of form and structure of story comes firsthand from the attempt to write a story, particularly if the student tries to match the *structure* of a myth or fairy tale, perhaps using realistic incidents from his own time. Writing should come after exposure to forms, for literature grows out of literature itself, and children should not be expected to compose in a vacuum. Story can be created in movements, shapes, and color, as well as in words. It may be composed of the images that make up a film.

Literary Forms Order Experience

The composition of original stories should, of course, be an integral part of the curriculum in literary studies. Children in the elementary school should write story more than discursive prose for it is through story that the child orders his experience and orients himself to the world. Children, as James Moffett says, "do all of their serious business in a play form. That is to say, it is a great mistake to regard their addiction to stories as mere childish pleasure seeking to be catered to until they have sobered up enough to reflect on life. They are already reflecting an enormous amount; we can't *stop* them from doing it. All adults have to do is recognize the function of their fun, and honor stories as a genuine mode of thought."* In *From Two to Five*, Chukovsky describes children who, deprived of fairy tales and fantasy, spontaneously spin their own as their method of coming to terms with the world.

Exposure to Literary Forms as Stimulus for Composition

Children may be helped toward precision and order in their process of ordering the world through language without loss of creativity and spontaneity. The selection and shaping that language involves, the choices between alternative expressions so that language will fit experience and give it life—these activities imply imaginative work. The teacher must be wise enough to find ways to channel verbal energy without binding it. Writing or composing orally on tape or dictating must be stimulated, nurtured, and guided with sympathy, tact, and a sense of purpose. Poetic patterns have been shown as necessary input in the process of freeing children to create their own poetry; story patterns have the same function. Providing the child with a pattern to give shape to his imaginings saves him hours of frustration; his creativity is aided rather than curtailed. Creation is facilitated by the use of technical conventions outside the individual that control his creative composition without suppressing it.

Inventing stories seems to be more difficult for a child than creating with paint or modeling materials, particularly if the child is asked to *write* a story. His vocabulary may be too limited to express his feelings, he may be held back by his lack of speed and skill in handwriting, his inhibitions about spelling, or his basic bewilderment about how to proceed. All too often children are told to write a story without sufficient prior motivation or stimulation in the form of models and materials. This is not to say that children

*James Moffett, *A Student-Centered Language Arts Curriculum, K-6: A Handbook for Teachers* (Boston: Houghton Mifflin, 1968), p. 118.

should be taught to copy or that they should be in competition with the professional and intimidated by him. Criticism that emphasizes literary form and structure as the means of shaping and ordering the imaginings of all writers, experienced or inexperienced, will help the young writer to see that he shares with all storytellers the same problems of composition and can only benefit from a consideration of their ways of dealing with these problems as he goes about setting down what necessarily must be his own personal interpretations of experience.

Impersonal forms provide structures into which children can project feeling unself-consciously. David Holbrook, the British educator who has had considerable success in freeing the most resistant children to write, favors the use of forms to release ideas and feelings.

> I felt the only way to achieve . . . expression was by using stimulant poems, passages, and themes which the child already recognized as means to the depersonalizing of his individual emotion—a way to that "third ground" which is a meeting-place between the "mind" of a community and his own. Such a depersonalized world, I have tried to suggest, exists in the sea-shanty, the folksong and the game rhyme. It also exists in such poetry as the Chinese poems translated by Arthur Waley. The fairy tale provides it, and so too, I think, do certain other conventional types of child's story—the story of exploration, for instance. And, it seems to me, that even the Wild Western may provide a half-serious, half-irresponsible world where self-identification may be indulged in.*

Children, in fact, turn naturally to literary forms and patterns they have encountered when they create stories of their own. Two psychologists conducted an extensive study in which they collected examples of the stories children tell and write. In *Children Tell Stories*, a book based on these studies, they reported that the imagined happenings from stories and pictures children had seen and heard figured largely in their representations of ordinary living. They created variants of fables and fairy tales, long adventure stories, and stories of ghosts and goblins. The children's stories, in their structure and use of symbol and imagery, showed striking similarities to literary archetypes: "of consuming oneself, of humor arising from incongruity and exaggeration, . . . of death and com-

---

*David Holbrook, *English for Maturity*, 2nd ed. (New York: Cambridge University Press, 1967), p. 115.

ing alive again . . . human relationships and hostile wishes and death."*

There must, then, be input before there can be output on the part of the child writer. Impressions and experiences may be unique but they require a convention for their expression in words.

Ideas of what originality is are often highly exaggerated; the best writers have always used the forms and conventions, even the ideas of those who came before, bringing their own individuality to their works. The child writer should be encouraged to do the same. He might rewrite a story using a different form, a myth as a story poem, say, or an adventure story as a play. He might write tales or story poems with contemporary settings that follow the pattern of old tales and ballads; the triad pattern of the fairy tales might be the form of a modern "realistic" story; the Cinderella story may be set down in modern terms; the hero's quest is not limited to ancient tales of romance and adventure, but may feature a youthful hero or heroine very like its young author; original tall tales may be created with the old ones as patterns; or young writers may create their own myths of origin along the lines of the myths of the primitives or by using the formula of Kipling's "just-so" stories.

Cooperative Composition

Group writing, like group discussion, should be encouraged. Compositions may be collective or individual in the group situation. The transition from collective to individual is likely to occur naturally as groups think up variations on a common theme, using each other's ideas as stimuli.

In a classroom with a healthy climate of encouragement and support, children gain much by reading each other's work, offering suggestions, giving each other help with word choice, spelling, and punctuation. Oral reading of one's own material gives it life and meaning that may be misinterpreted when a reader is confronted with a written form that falls short of presenting precisely what the youthful author meant to say. His own voice adds the inflections and intonations that his pen was too inexperienced to provide. Moreover, flaws in design are detected more readily when material is read aloud.

The children should be allowed to work as long as they need to on their rough drafts: revising, refurbishing, revamping. The

*Evelyn Goodenough Pitcher and Ernst Prelinger, *Children Tell Stories: An Analysis of Fantasy* (New York: International Universities Press, 1963), pp. 8-9.

teacher circulates, offering assistance to groups and individuals when it is asked for or when he recognizes the need. If the children are fully stimulated and prepared to write, and allowed to work cooperatively, frustrated pencil-chewing will give way more readily to eager pencil-pushing.

When putting words down on paper presents difficulties for young children, they should be encouraged to compose their stories orally, dictating them to an older student or to the teacher, or recording them on a tape that they can listen to, edit, and revise.

The "writer's workshop" in the classroom is preferable to lonely literary endeavors that are the result of homework assignments. The young writer requires aid and encouragement, both from his peers and his teacher, and this is forthcoming if he works at his compositions in a classroom climate of acceptance and sympathy for his efforts.

Case Histories in Composition

One fourth-grade class had read, in poetry and prose, the exploits of Robin Hood until they knew him and each of his merry men as old friends. In groups they set out to write their own episodes of the Robin Hood story, showing him and his men engaged in new adventures. Interest was high and the project continued for many days, resulting in a mimeographed booklet of some never-before recorded adventures of Robin Hood that would have delighted Howard Pyle as much as it did its authors.

A sixth-grade class concentrated on the short story. The teacher read aloud to them a wide selection of different types of stories: Poe's "The Tell-Tale Heart," O. Henry's "The Ransom of Red Chief," Saroyan's "Locomotive 88," Quentin Reynold's "A Secret for Two," Ray Bradbury's "Fever Dream," Ellis Parker Butler's "Pigs Is Pigs," and many more. The children themselves found others that they enjoyed in searches through library anthologies, prepared them, and read them aloud to the class. In addition, they listened to recordings of short stories read by professionals.

Together, working in groups, the children evolved a description of short story technique: few characters, economy of expression, early establishment of setting and situation, and so on. They then discussed possible subjects for short stories, with many students working out character sketches, settings, outlines of plots, and situations cooperatively. The writing took place in class. The important first paragraphs were tested on others and revised again and again to suit the requirements of the pupil-critics who were now in command of much that constitutes effective short story technique. Final dog-eared drafts were polished and read aloud; then last corrections were made. Proofreading was an important part of the project: the work had to be technically correct, since it was to be published for distribution among other classes and among parents. A bound copy, complete with card, was placed with the library's collection of short stories for circulation.

A *fourth grade* had read many myths of origin, particularly those found in the mythology of North American Indians: "Why the Robin Has a Red Breast," "How the Rabbit Got His Short Tail," and many others. Then they composed their own, dictating into a tape recorder marvelous explanations of why the grass is green, why the sky is blue, why dogs bark, and why birds sing.

A *third grade* delighted in the teacher's reading of the tall tales that tell of the exploits of Paul Bunyan and Pecos Bill. Then they wrote some taller tales of their own.

First graders composed tiny tales in the manner of nursery tales like "The Three Billy Goats Gruff" and "The Three Pigs," using children like themselves as their chief characters; and fierce dogs, threatening witches, and snakes as their antagonists.

Mechanical Skills

The problem of honing and polishing mechanical skills is minimized when children work cooperatively, with excitement, on something they really want to do. Not every literary form encountered will provide the necessary stimulus for a class project, of course, and it is not advisable that it should. Some types of stories will enthrall and absorb more than others, and these will be the ones the children will most want to try themselves.

No author writes well, particularly as to the mechanics of writing, unless he has an audience. When the children write for each other, the audience is ready-made. If they know that others are interested in their ideas, they will work to perfect the skills necessary for effective communication. Certainly they will write more eagerly if they know their work will be shared by sympathetic readers and not merely found fault with by the red pencil. When composition comes first, handwriting, punctuation, spelling, and the like are put in their place—one of importance in facilitating communication, but always as part of an editing process, coming after having something to say and someone to say it to. Working with small groups and individuals, the teacher gives help with mechanical skills where it is needed. In every class there is such a wide range of ability in the use of language that it is a fruitless, yawn-inspiring endeavor to drill mechanical skills, the use of commas and capitals, spelling, and the like, to an entire class at once. More can be accomplished and more quickly with a few or with one pupil at a time. The child can read aloud from his imperfect prose and the teacher can show him how, with punctuation and the like, to give his words voice, and influence the poor speller to admit that, if he wants readers to share his ideas, he must use more familiar spellings.

The practice of having children write and "hand in" a composition for the teacher to grade is of dubious value as a learning experience. Confronted with a page of prose that seems to require nothing less than major surgery, it is the rare teacher who can refrain from the use of the correcting pencil. The child's next attempt at writing, if he makes one, is likely to repeat the same errors or show signs of inhibition as the author retreats into terse or insipid means of expression in an effort to minimize his errors and reduce the amount of red that will appear on his paper. When the teacher does read the children's offerings, it will be more fruitful for all concerned if, as he reads, he jots down notes for his own use in planning individual and small group lessons in areas that require improvement. One child may need help in constructing complete sentences or in subordinating ideas; another may have personal problems in spelling and usage that warrant special instruction; there may be indications in the work of several children that they would profit from special assistance in using words more precisely or in developing general ideas with elaborative detail. Occasionally the teacher will note a problem so widespread that it warrants a lesson for the entire class.

If the teacher does write a comment on a child's work, it should be a reaction to the ideas that he finds there, to indicate that the writer has communicated something of his experience, feelings, hopes, interests, wishes, or whatever he has tried to express. If, for example, a young writer has tried, in halting prose, to describe his delight in a new pet, the teacher's comment will show that he has "read" him if it goes something like this: "Your new cat sounds a lot like mine. I'd like to hear more about him!" Work with the student writer on the mechanics of his written expression will not be ignored but deferred. It can take place in a personal conversation, and what the writer has tried to communicate should take precedence over his mechanical problems of communication.

Another questionable practice for classroom composition is teacher acceptance of random outpourings for their own sake or for the sake of "self-expression." The therapeutic value of such excesses has not been proven, and, although the teacher may pride himself on accepting without question whatever the child writes, he is not helping him to grow in effectual use of language, a developmental growth that requires shaping, molding, guiding, and instructing.

Publication

Some children may prefer, for a number of reasons, not to share their literary efforts, even with the teacher, or at least not until he has proven himself a sympathetic audience. But most children will delight in seeing their work in print in classroom publications. It is always easier to write if one has an audience in mind, and the tedious tasks of editing and revising become not only bearable but essential when a writer knows that he is perfecting his work to facilitate the communication of his ideas to others.

An excellent form of publication that appeals particularly to children is the creation of their own, simply-bound books. These may be produced as class projects or they may contain the work of individuals or small groups. They may be illustrated or decorated and include title pages, dedications, and tables of contents. Class anthologies of original stories, ballads, haiku, cinquain, and the like may be prepared throughout the year. A sympathetic librarian is likely to accept the books for circulation. Older children may create original stories and picture books for children in the primary grades. The stories of younger children may be printed out by the teacher on charts or sheets of oak tag for room displays. Stories and poems may be put on tape as a way to publish and preserve them for others' enjoyment. One class might share their stories and poems with another, presenting them in bound editions or staging prepared readings of them. A class newspaper or magazine is an excellent way to publish compositions of all kinds. Another form of publication is the "talking" newspaper or magazine, with the children recording on tape pieces they have written or otherwise composed.

Oral and Pictorial Composition as Part of the Critical Process

Composition, whether in words, the movements of dance or mime, in paint or film, is essential exercise for the imagination.

It may also be seen as an integral part of the process of literary criticism. Creative responses to literature—the acting out of key scenes in stories, miming to the rhythm of a poem, painting or drawing impressions of settings and characters, the creation of original dramas, paintings from the imagination, and mimes not directly related to a particular story or poem—are part of literary criticism. The groups of children who prepare a story for dramatization, for instance, are involved in a critical analysis of the structure of the story, deciding upon the key scenes to be dramatized and a coherent sequence for their presentation. Those who compose an original mime or drama must consider their story in terms of its beginning, middle, and end. How will the problem or conflict be introduced? How will it be resolved? How will the characters interrelate in the development of the plot? Thus, composition in other forms than words may embody a number of aspects central to the practice of elementary literary criticism, among them: enjoyment in experiencing, imaginative interpretation of individual works, creative composition, realization of form and structure in story.

The Use of Film in the
Elementary Literature Curriculum

All of the aspects of archetypal criticism that apply to printed stories, such as the concept of basic story "shapes" and the quest of the hero, apply as well to stories on film suitable for children as they do to stories in print. Children will be encouraged to draw upon their film experiences, in and out of school, during discussions of literary principles. Just as they can be taught to read printed stories perceptively, noting point of view, mood, tone, how characters are developed and how they interrelate, and the like, so they can be taught to "read" film with greater perception. The critical principle that stories must be first grasped as entities applies both to filmed and printed stories.

"Literature" on film and literature in print have a number of things in common, although each medium does make use of techniques that are unique to it. The film, with unusual juxtaposition of images, variations of length and angle of shots, and the like, can create a metaphorical language of association without using words. Films have a concentrated power of archetypal expression—the intensity of their symbolism is unmatched. Both types of creative expression employ images and symbols in similar ways: darkness and shadow symbolize the evil, menacing, or threatening; light and color are associated with their opposites. Landscapes and natural surroundings as well as weather are powerful images in creating mood and atmosphere. When the film-maker chooses to tell a story, his structural problems are similar to those of the author to the extent that he must find ways to begin, develop, and end his story. Since stories come in a limited number of basic shapes, the filmed story falls into one of the categories of comedy, romance, tragedy, or irony. The dialectical and cyclical structures of imagery are common to all types of literature. Thus, for variety, for enjoyment, and because the film is an important aspect of literature, particularly today, filmed literature should take its place with print in the elementary curriculum.

The composition of films by the children encompasses several aspects of the process of literary criticism. It involves a creative response as well as an analysis of the elements of story: character development, setting, tone, plot structure, point of view, and the like. If a printed story is to be adapted for filming, children must become aware of the story in terms of its structure; deciding, for instance, what scenes and characters are essential to the recreation of the story on film and which are not. When the project involves the creation of an original movie, the storytellers must consider how to structure their story: how and where it should begin, how and by whom the plot will be developed, how it should be ended. Usually, the first step in the creation of a film is the designing of a story board, a sequence of sketches that tell the story pictorially with instructions for the length and angle of each shot included in a caption. The story-board technique has obvious possibilities for teaching the children to trace a sequence of events and for helping them to see story in terms of structure and form. As a form of structural analysis this is exciting as well as profitable and it leads naturally into the shooting of films by the children themselves.

The use of filmed and printed literature together makes possible another form of literary criticism. Cross-media comparisons may be made between stories told in print and the films based on them.* The children will draw many conclusions about the unique characteristics of each media. Films, for example, do not require descriptions of either the characters' appearance or the setting since the viewer sees these details for himself. In printed literature we are told what the character feels and thinks; film is more suited to showing us his physical reactions. Many children will find it interesting to discuss the relative merits of each medium. In a classroom where printed literature is a lively art, there will be none who see film as a substitute for it.

*One example is *Evan's Corner* by Elizabeth Starr Hill. A film based on the book is available from BFA Educational Media, 2211 Michigan Ave., Santa Monica, Calif. 90404.

Chapter 9

A Postscript

Mathematics, music, physical education, social studies, science, and art all have their places in the elementary curriculum. They are firmly established as subjects of study, their content and methods of instruction receive serious consideration. It is not so with literature. Yet literature, of all man's creations, is one of the greatest sources of nourishment for developing minds and imaginations.

It has the capacity to delight; it is meant to be enjoyed, and children deserve every chance to revel in its pleasures. Literature is a humanistic study and studies in the humanities are essential to our survival in a technological world where things can easily become more important than people. Literature is a civilizing influence. Because it deals with human experience, because it has everything to do with people—their actions, their needs and desires—literature can show us both sides of the coin: What it means to be truly human and what it means to be inhumane. Because it is an art made of words, literature develops from and extends the aspect of man that separates him from all other animals, his language.

It is surely time to consider seriously the literary education of young children. It must be an education worthy of the name. It must be significant and systematic, with a sense of continuity; it cannot be piecemeal, but instead a piecing together of details that fit gradually into a meaningful design.

As we have seen, Northrop Frye's revolutionary literary theory can be effectively put to use to make the earliest study of literature significant. Because it delineates the structural principles of literature, his scheme provides a means of unifying and integrating experience with literary works. It allows the student to look beyond this story or that poem to a vision of a whole that is greater than even the greatest of its parts. Surely the ability to see relationships

116

and make connections is the essence of education in any field of study. Without a structure, experience is fragmentary and fleeting, a series of chance encounters that offer little in the way of genuine enlightenment.

It is important to emphasize again how inappropriate it would be to teach a complex literary theory directly to children. A knowledge of it enables *the teacher* to lead young critics to discover for themselves how literature works. It provides a method for approaching literary studies with purpose.

When literary criticism is treated seriously, we find that literature is placed firmly where it belongs: at the center of the elementary curriculum. The study of literature in all its aspects is the road to literacy. No detours are necessary. The child critic listens in wonder, reads with delight, responds to art with art. Of course, there can be no satisfactory results without commitment and a total commitment at that. Literature *is* the language art. All the other "language arts" are developed from and through it.

Unfortunately, it is radical today to insist that a program to develop literacy can and should be centered in literature, fiction and poetry in particular. Yet, children in large numbers have not thrived on instructional diets that serve up imaginative literature only as dessert. These children have turned to television to satisfy their desire for fantasy, their need to hear language that jingles, rhymes, and sings. For many of them reading is only an onerous exercise confined to classrooms.

Literature is the richest possible source of reading material. There is something for everyone among the thousands of children's books so readily available. There are stories and poems to echo every human feeling: desire for excitement and adventure, curiosity, fear, loneliness, jealousy, anger, hope, compassion, frustration, tenderness, rage. Feeling comes first.

Children want to read what makes them laugh or cry, shiver and gasp. They must have stories and poems that reflect what they themselves have felt. They need the thrill of imagining, of being for a time in some hero's shoes for a spine-tingling adventure. They deserve to experience the delight and amazement that comes with hearing language that puns and plays. For children reading must be equated with imagining, wondering, reacting feelingly. If it is not, we should not be surprised if they refuse to read.

A light touch must accompany all our efforts to teach literary criticism to children. Too heavy a hand, however scholarly, is as undesirable as it is unnecessary. Literature is an art and art is first of all to be experienced and savored. Even so, experience alone is not an adequate teacher. The study of literature takes place in the school and educators must concern themselves with growth and development. A knowledgeable adult who can guide this development is essential. As defined here, literary criticism is an all inclusive concept that includes experiencing literature, responding to it and creating it. Its practice does not depend upon commercially prepared programs or rigid timetables. No textbooks are necessary. What is needed to teach literary criticism is literature itself, genuine literature of all kinds and in great quantities. In this wealth of material all children will find some things that will compel them to listen, to read for themselves, to talk about what they have read, and to try to create literature of their own. An informed teacher is there to plan and structure presentations, to ask the right questions, to listen, to inspire, and to guide every creative effort.

The development of language ability, whether it be reading or writing, is a cumulative development. Unlike other studies, it develops from the inside out. When words engage our feelings and imaginations, we are motivated to read them. When our feelings and imaginings are stimulated, we have a need to use language to express them. That is why literature must play a major role in the development of our ability to make use of language. Words are powerful magic and nowhere is this magic more evident than in the language of literature. Literature, in partnership with the teacher who believes in its power, will work to produce those who are truly literate, readers and writers who are aware of the potential of language: its nature, its uses, its joy.

Bibliography

Selected Reference Books

Arbuthnot, May Hill, and others. *The Arbuthnot Anthology of Children's Literature*, 3rd ed. Glenview, Ill.: Scott, Foresman and Company, 1971.

> An excellent selection of writing for children. Included in this volume is "Time for Poetry," one of the finest collections of poems for young people.

Arbuthnot, May Hill, and Sutherland, Zena. *Children and Books*. Glenview, Ill.: Scott, Foresman and Company, 1972.

> A basic source of information for teachers and parents. Includes discussion of all varieties of children's literature, criteria for evaluation and selection, methods of presentation, resources for further study.

Chukovsky, Kornei. *From Two to Five*, trans. by Miriam Morton. Berkeley: University of California Press, 1963.

> A Russian poet's sensitive discussion of young children's language and thought. Emphasizes the importance of imaginative literature in a child's development.

Frye, Northrop. *Anatomy of Criticism: Four Essays*. Princeton: Princeton University Press, 1957.

> This revolutionary book gives "a synoptic view of the scope, theory, principles, and techniques of literary criticism." An attempt to establish order in a disorderly field, it sets forth principles to inform the teaching of literature.

Frye, Northrop. *The Educated Imagination*. Bloomington: Indiana University Press, 1964.

> The distinguished literary critic discusses, in six lectures originally broadcast by the Canadian Broadcasting Corporation, the central role played by literature in the development of the imag-

ination. In one of the lectures, Frye presents his views on the order and content appropriate in literary studies for children.

Frye, Northrop, supervisory ed. *Literature: Uses of the Imagination.* New York: Harcourt Brace Jovanovich, 1973.

> Eleven pupil anthologies with accompanying teacher's manuals provide a sequential program for the study of literature in grades seven through twelve. An innovative program based upon the literary theory of Northrop Frye.

Frye, Northrop. *The Stubborn Structure: Essays on Criticism and Society.* Ithaca: Cornell University Press, 1970.

> A collection of essays and lectures dealing with the contexts of literary criticism and specific studies in literature. Of particular interest to teachers is an essay on the teaching of literature, "Elementary Teaching and Elemental Scholarship."

Frye, Northrop. *The Well-Tempered Critic.* Bloomington: Indiana University Press, 1963.

> Three essays dealing with styles of language and the teaching of literature. Emphasizes the importance of poetry as the basis of a literary education.

Holbrook, David. *English for Maturity*, 2nd ed. New York: Cambridge University Press, 1967.

> A British educator's plea for fresh and vital approaches to the teaching of English. Although the book discusses teaching in secondary schools, its sound pedagogy is applicable and adaptable to elementary classrooms.

Johnson, Edna; Sickels, Evelyn R.; and Sayers, Frances Clarke. *Anthology of Children's Literature.* Boston: Houghton Mifflin, 1970.

> A distinguished collection of the poetry and prose written for children. The brief, well-written scholarly introductions to each section are an outstanding feature of this fine anthology.

Koch, Kenneth. *Rose, Where Did You Get That Red?* New York: Vintage Books, 1973.

> A poet describes his enlightened methods of teaching great poetry to children. Includes examples of the original poetry students wrote in response to inspired teaching of fine literature.

Koch, Kenneth. *Wishes, Lies and Dreams.* New York: Chelsea House, 1970.

> Using numerous examples of children's work, the poet tells how he went into city classrooms to "free children to write poetry."

Langer, Susanne K. *Philosophy in a New Key.* New York: New American Library, 1948.

> This book includes a stimulating discussion of discursive and non-discursive language. In the chapter "Language," the author gives support to the thesis that the expressive use of language precedes the utilitarian.

Moffett, James. *A Student-Centered Language Arts Curriculum, K-6: A Handbook for Teachers.* Boston: Houghton Mifflin, 1968.

> An educator sets out his provocative ideas, tested in classrooms, for teaching all aspects of language to children.

Odland, Norine. *Teaching Literature in the Elementary School.* Urbana, Ill.: National Council of Teachers of English, 1969.

> The author reviews relevant research, curriculum trends, teaching materials, the judgments of recognized experts in the field, reports and findings from various national committees and commissions in an attempt to answer the question "Where are we?" The answer, unfortunately, is: We have a long way to go before we can say we teach literature in the elementary school.

Opie, Iona and Peter. *The Lore and Language of School Children.* New York: Oxford University Press, 1959.

> A fascinating record of the school child's strange and primitive culture including innumerable rhymes and chants, catcalls, stock jokes, riddles, and slang epithets. Comprehensive, scholarly, and exceedingly readable.

Parker, Elizabeth Ann. *Teaching the Reading of Fiction.* New York: Teachers College Press, 1969.

> A handbook for teachers that offers concrete suggestions for teaching the unique "reading skills" appropriate to the reading of fiction.

Pitcher, Evelyn Goodenough, and Prelinger, Ernst. *Children Tell Stories: An Analysis of Fantasy.* New York: International Universities Press, 1963.

> This collection of stories, written by boys and girls from two to five, brings to light the subjective experience of little children.

Wolsch, Robert. *Poetic Composition Through the Grades.* New York: Teachers College Press, 1970.

> A program to develop poetic composition that is built upon the conviction that poetry is an essential ingredient in the development of literacy and the imagination.

Index to Children's Books and Stories

Index to Poems

About the Author

Glenna Davis Sloan has long been interested in children and the place of literature in their education—as an elementary and junior high school teacher and later as English department chairman, all in the North York, Ontario, school system. She has contributed to reading, literature, and language arts series for elementary, junior and senior high schools published in both Canada and the United States and has written several articles on teaching literature to children. Educated at the University of Toronto and Teachers College, Columbia University, she is presently an associate professor in the Department of Early Childhood and Elementary Education at Queens College of the City University of New York and lives on Long Island with her husband and young son.

Other Teachers College Press books
on teaching literature to children

THE TRAGIC MODE IN CHILDREN'S LITERATURE
Carolyn T. Kingston

Though literature for children often avoids dealing with the tragic sense of life, there are some notable exceptions. These the author explores here, concentrating on their moments of rejection, entrapment, sensitivity, war, and loss, and on how such realistic fiction can be used with eight- to twelve-year-old children. (1974)

BEYOND WORDS: MYSTICAL FANCY IN CHILDREN'S LITERATURE
James E. Higgins

Here creativity in literature for children is evaluated as the writer's ability to show respect for the "innate rights" of the child. The author shows how books, and which books in particular, of mystical fancy appeal to the "inner child." (1970)

TEACHING THE READING OF FICTION
Elizabeth A. Parker

The author addresses the question of what abilities should be developed in students of the upper elementary grades for their successful reading of prose fiction, both in school and beyond. Calling fiction a "unique way of knowing," she offers practical proposals for leading children into that world of story. (1969)

USING LITERATURE WITH YOUNG CHILDREN
Leland B. Jacobs, General Editor

These ten essays by early childhood educators on ways to enhance children's enjoyment of literature include Leland Jacobs on telling stories, Constance Carr McCutcheon on evaluating children's experience with literature, others on choral speaking, reading aloud, dramatizing literature, and relating literature to the child's other experiences. (1965; 5th printing, 1974)